ANDREY RUBLEV

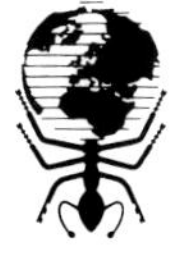

Covering one of the most fascinating yet misunderstood periods in history, the MEDIEVAL LIVES series presents medieval people, concepts and events, drawing on political and social history, philosophy, material culture (art, architecture and archaeology) and the history of science. These books are global and wide-ranging in scope, encompassing both Western and non-Western subjects, and span the fifth to the fifteenth centuries, tracing significant developments from the collapse of the Roman Empire onwards.

SERIES EDITOR: Deirdre Jackson

Albertus Magnus and the World of Nature *Irven M. Resnick and Kenneth F. Kitchell Jr*

Alle Thyng Hath Tyme: Time and Medieval Life *Gillian Adler and Paul Strohm*

Andrey Rublev: The Artist and His World *Robin Milner-Gulland*

The Art of Anatomy in Medieval Europe *Taylor McCall*

Christine de Pizan: Life, Work, Legacy *Charlotte Cooper-Davis*

Margery Kempe: A Mixed Life *Anthony Bale*

ANDREY RUBLEV

The Artist and His World

ROBIN MILNER-GULLAND

REAKTION BOOKS

To the memory of Professors D. S. Likhachov and D. D. Obolensky

Published by Reaktion Books Ltd
Unit 32, Waterside
44–48 Wharf Road
London N1 7UX, UK
www.reaktionbooks.co.uk

First published 2023
Copyright © Robin Milner-Gulland 2023

Printed and bound in India by Replika Press Pvt. Ltd

A catalogue record for this book is available from the British Library

ISBN 978 1 78914 680 6

CONTENTS

NOTE ON TRANSLITERATION

As always with books on Russian themes, transliteration of names presents particular problems. Following other books I have written or translated for Reaktion, I have used the 'British system' devised by W. K. Matthews, which gives a good idea of pronunciation for non-Russian speakers. Most proper names are better rendered through transliteration than translation ('Andrey' rather than 'Andrew'; 'Kirill' rather than 'Cyril'). But I make an exception for St Sergius, future patron saint of Russia, who stands close to the heart of our narrative (rather than using his Slavonic name 'Sergiy' or its modern version 'Sergey'). Also, perhaps arbitrarily, I refer to 'St Joseph' of Volokolamsk and 'St Stephen' of Perm, and refer to two princes and an abbot as 'Alexander', not 'Aleksandr'. We spell 'Kiev' in the historically accepted manner, not according to the twentieth-century transliteration 'Kyiv'. Rus refers to the pre-Tatar Russian principalities, some of them in modern Ukraine or Belarus.

With the name 'Rublev' itself a curious problem arises. In Russian as spoken today, his name is pronounced 'Rublyov'. At some point in the Middle Ages the vowel 'ye', when stressed, normally acquired the pronunciation 'yo', and it is impossible for us now to know what he called himself or was called. Note too that monks and nuns took on a new name; whatever Rublev's birth name was, it cannot have been Andrey.

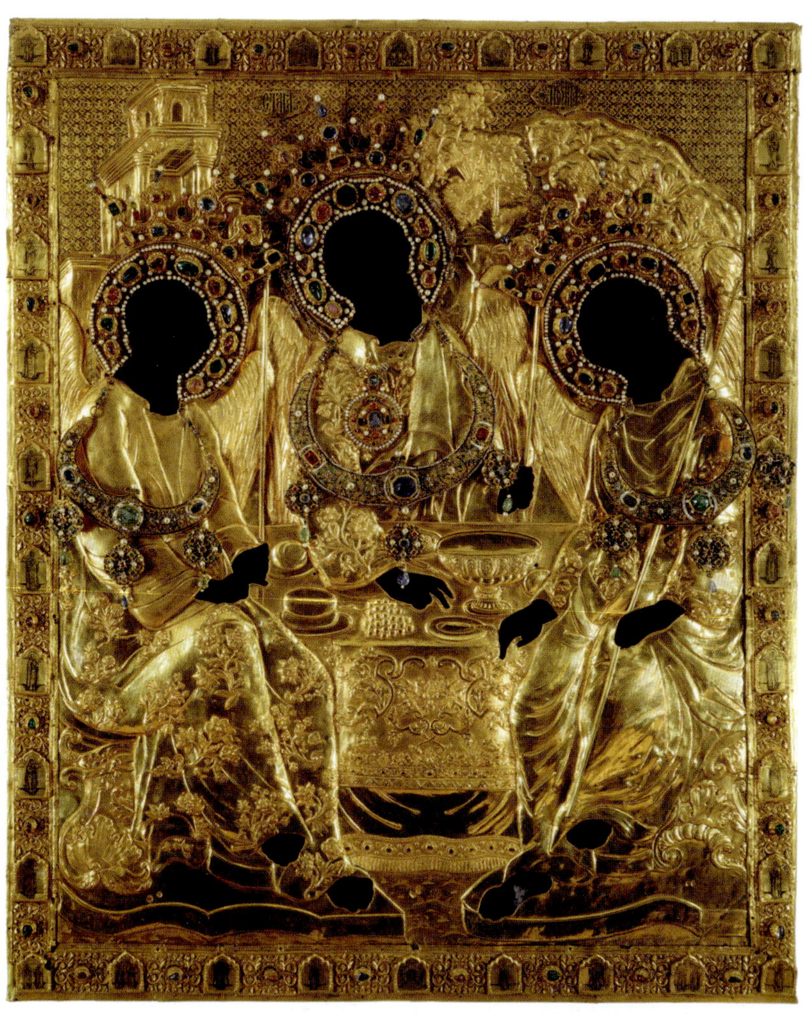

1 Casing (*oklad*) for the *Old Testament Trinity* icon (late 16th–early 17th century). This silver, gold and jewelled casing was provided by Boris Godunov; Tsar Mikhail added the half-moon pendants of gold and enamel; in the 18th century another layer of silver was added to cover the icon completely.

Introduction

How is one to compose the biography of an artist who was undoubtedly of the first importance, but about whom almost nothing is known with any certainty? The task would be worthy of a Borges mystification. Everything that seems established can slip through the fingers. In the case of Rublev, we have two firm references to work he did in his lifetime, in the Trinity Chronicle under the years 1405 and 1408 (the important MS of the Trinity Chronicle itself was destroyed in the 1812 fire of Moscow, but luckily could be reconstructed by the modern scholar M. Prisyolkov). We do not know where or when he was born (though no doubt in the 1360s) or how he spent his first thirty or forty years, but it seems we know the date of his death: 29 January 1430. Or do we? This was copied by an eighteenth-century antiquarian from a gravestone in the courtyard of the Moscow Andronikov Monastery at a spot that was later built over. That note itself was not preserved, but was in turn copied. Not surprisingly, many modern scholars are unwilling to accept it as evidence, though I do.

Even his surname – unusual in his time – is problematic, and it is uncertain how he pronounced it. The paintings securely attributed to Rublev, few in number, have almost all suffered damage of various kinds, while other questions of attribution seem neverending, despite meticulous scholarly efforts. All other sources relating to him – of varying reliability – postdate 1430.

To these problems we return in due course as appropriate, but they may help to explain why no previous volume on him (so far as I know) has ever appeared in English. The closest has been a detailed study of his most famous icon by the Swiss Orthodox monk and theologian Gabriel Bunge, translated by Andrew Louth (2007). At this point it seems incumbent on the present author to show his hand. One could hardly presume to match Fr Bunge's theological knowledge and insights, or those of several other contemporary experts; nor would one wish to (though in discussing a religious artist, matters of religion cannot help but be of major importance). Some knowledge of the Bible and the basic tenets of Christianity are assumed; beyond that, in approaching Rublev I have taken a viewpoint that attempts to position his art and the art around him within a cultural-historical framework – one that reaches into our own times, indeed. It is a complicated and (I think) interesting framework, worth some attention. But I believe that in appreciating Rublev in our, or any, age, one cannot help but start from the immediate joy and uplift that his great works inspire, and trust that any further knowledge of his life, times and works will serve to enhance this. To that end we pay special attention to the visual material in this volume, and do our best to explain it in context.

That said, what can a concise book on Rublev mean to a modern readership? To Western Europeans, it probably evokes one of two mental constructs, reaching somewhat different groups. To churchgoers of several persuasions, it will no doubt summon up the ubiquitous reproductions of the icon studied by Bunge known as the *Old Testament Trinity*, more properly the *Hospitality of Abraham*, now displayed at the Tretyakov Gallery in Moscow. To quote Canon Donald Allchin, 'Rublev's great icon of the Holy Trinity turns up everywhere, in Protestant places of prayer no less than Catholic ones . . . No-one has promoted this cult of icons. It has been spontaneous.'[1]

To another constituency, *Andrei Rublev* is the title of one of the half-dozen major films made by Andrey Tarkovsky (1966) and known to everyone with a serious interest in cinema. It is composed of a series of episodes presenting an imagined view of the painter's life and times – a curious and daring endeavour, since Tarkovsky left himself open to attacks from various quarters. As is often pointed out, it is more a meditation on the role of the artist than a historical recreation, and its original version was called *The Passion According to Andrey* (the director's own name too, of course, and that of his close colleague and collaborator A. S. Mikhalkov-Konchalovsky).

For Russians, steeped in their own history, the name Rublev conjures up different trains of thought and mental images, some no doubt over-romanticized; they are likely to be aware that he was canonized as an Orthodox saint in 1988. There are also strongly held positions and disagreements among the art (and general) historians who have made Rublev their specialism. While taking these into account, I have tried to come to any conclusions on the balance of probabilities, not wanting to bore the reader by revisiting all such disputes.

Russians anyhow, believers or not, are likely to have a familiarity with the background of Eastern or Orthodox ('Pravoslavny', 'right-praising' to Slavs) Christianity that Western readers – even those well versed in Catholic or Protestant history – may lack. So a brief outline of some of its special features may be useful. As with other Christian denominations, its bedrock of belief is the Bible, but unlike in the West, where for centuries the only authoritative biblical text was in Latin, Orthodoxy 'devolved' its Bible to various speech communities. The Slav nations, whose colloquial languages were then close enough to be inter-comprehensible, inherited what became known as 'Church Slavonic' from the activity of saints Cyril and Methodius in the ninth century CE (first in Moravia, thereafter in Bulgaria). They came from Thessaloniki, where the Greek and Slav linguistic worlds met, and were evidently bilingual. When in the following century, 988/9, the Russians underwent official conversion – actually there were Christians in Kiev earlier – the written word effectively came in as an accompaniment to the new system of faith; an aura of sacredness attended it, as it did its equally new pictorial and musical methods.

Authority too was to some extent decentralized in Orthodoxy. The Church as a whole was divided into the five early patriarchates: Rome, Alexandria, Antioch, Constantinople and Jerusalem (as recognized at the Council of Ephesus in 431). Later, others were added (Moscow in 1589). During the period that is our main concern, the three patriarchates under Islamic rule were attenuated in their significance. The Patriarch of Rome – the pope – held all Western Europe until the Reformation, and became known as 'Catholic', that is, universal. In the east, the Oecumenical (relating to the whole inhabited world) Patriarch was that of Constantinople, or Byzantium as it is usually called in the West, accepted as 'first among equals' – thus not pretending to the total authority of the pope. Subdivisions of patriarchates were under the authority of Metropolitans (as was Russia, during part of the fourteenth century subdivided into 'Great' and 'Little' Russia); below them were dioceses, which often maintained local traditions.

The seat of a bishop, East or West, is called a cathedral, but so is the main church (*sobor*) of an Orthodox monastery. The characteristic basilican (rectangular) form of a large church was scarcely known in Russia until the eighteenth century: churches there sported a central dome, and often subsidiary ones. On sacred terminology, note that the Virgin Mary is always known in the East as the 'Mother of God' and her Assumption as 'Dormition' (falling asleep). Doctrine was settled at ecumenical councils, of which there were seven, up to 787 (when icons were reaffirmed). Thereafter the Western church held a good many more (during which the doctrine of Purgatory was established); the East held fewer, though including the Council of Constantinople (1341–51), upholding the teaching of St Gregory Palamas on Hesychasm (see Chapter Five). The churches' drift apart hardened into schism in 1054. Several unsuccessful attempts have since been made to heal it; but the breach was greatly widened when Westerners of the Fourth Crusade sacked Constantinople, desecrated it in various ways and occupied it from 1204 to 1261.

The ordinary clergy of the Eastern Church are married. In Russian villages, the priest would live like his parishioners, tilling the soil. By contrast, bishops are unmarried, thus recruited from monasteries (unless a priest's wife has died or become a nun). We return to the monastic life below, but should note that Orthodoxy does not have separate monastic orders. All services, save where a bishop delivers a sermon, are sung, unaccompanied. This is no mere quirk of tradition: human voices alone are worthy to accompany the imagined and simultaneous singing of angels. Such a concept no doubt goes back to the central building of Orthodoxy, the 'Great Church', Santa Sophia (Holy Wisdom) in Constantinople, with its choirs well over a hundred strong and a wonderful play of light in its vast golden dome. The passage of the Primary Chronicle describing the reaction of emissaries from Vladimir I to the 'Greeks' is much quoted, sometimes in sentimental contexts, but bears repeating: 'They took us to where they serve their God, and we did not know whether we were on heaven or earth, for on earth there is no such spectacle or beauty … we know only that God is there among people, and their service is better than in all other lands. We cannot forget that beauty.'

The early musical notation (neumes) cannot now be deciphered, though elaborate melismas were a characteristic feature of them, but icons and wall paintings are still with us and can speak directly of the Orthodox idea of beauty. It would be a crass mistake to think of them as no more than devotional objects.

This is the moment to say something about the sources at our disposal, aside from the buildings, books and paintings themselves. With one remarkable exception (a letter), these fall into two categories: saints' lives and chronicles. Saints' lives, relatively laconic, simple and unemotional in pre-Tatar days, tended to become more rhetorically adorned as time went on (to some extent taking as an example the Serbian royal lives of the twelfth and thirteenth centuries), but within the rhetoric plenty of factual material can be found, though with copying and recopying political bias often creeps in. Old Russian chronicles are a rich source of information. After the solitary Primary Chronicle (1110s, drawing on earlier records), from which later chronicles derive, chronicles became numerous, compiled at both princely courts and major monasteries from notes that must have been systematically kept, and generally commemorating some significant event. Sometimes they have a political tendency, often in favour of a particular city, and we may well see the same event narrated from various points of view. Their tone differs considerably: some are coherent narratives (such as that of Galicia), some very down-to-earth (for example, the several Novgorod chronicles), whereas the Trinity Chronicle – instigated by the head of the Church, Metropolitan Kiprian, at the Trinity Monastery, on which more below – attempts an all-Russian perspective. But in essence a chronicle is a great compendium, a collage of different materials, or (as the modern poet Velimir Khlebnikov could have put it) a 'supertale'. Such works are generally very precise on recording the construction of major churches, which perhaps fill the role monuments would have had elsewhere. It is wonderful that many (up to the eighteenth century) have survived, in a land of wooden buildings prone to fire, frequent invasions and civil strife.

How then do we reliably know anything about Rublev? Two commissions he undertook with others, one in Moscow, one in Vladimir, are laconically recorded, as has been mentioned, in the Trinity Chronicle. Beyond that, there are brief references in an extended edition of the life of St Sergius produced by the itinerant monk and biographer Pakhomiy the Serb in the 1450s from the original by the learned writer Yepifaniy; also in the life of Sergius's successor as abbot, Nikon, again by Pakhomiy. In the second half of the fifteenth century a major Church figure, St Joseph of Volokolamsk, wrote glowingly about him and collected his icons. Thereafter we have a famous reference in the 'Council of 100 Chapters' (1551), prescribing that any 'Trinity' icon should follow 'ancient models, as the Greek icon painters painted, and as painted Andrey Rublev and other greatly-famed icon-painters'. Lastly, before he fades from the historical record, there is the seventeenth-century 'Tale of the Holy Icon-Painters', with the vital piece of information that the 'Trinity' was made to commemorate St Sergius. Thereafter, though not forgotten, he becomes a figure of myth.

This comes partly through ignorance, but more importantly from a quality affecting icons themselves: the linseed oil with which they are varnished darkens gradually over time, to the point where they can only dimly be discerned. Wall paintings, too, become obscured with candle smoke. Revered icons could be, and often were, overpainted – modern restorers may have to remove several layers of overpainting to reach the original, with sometimes astonishing results. Equally, a notable icon might be covered with a repoussé *oklad*, or case, which could itself be a work of art (this happened to the *Old Testament Trinity*; illus. 1). These could be richly decorated; usually the hands and face on the original surface were left visible to worshippers, slowly growing darker.

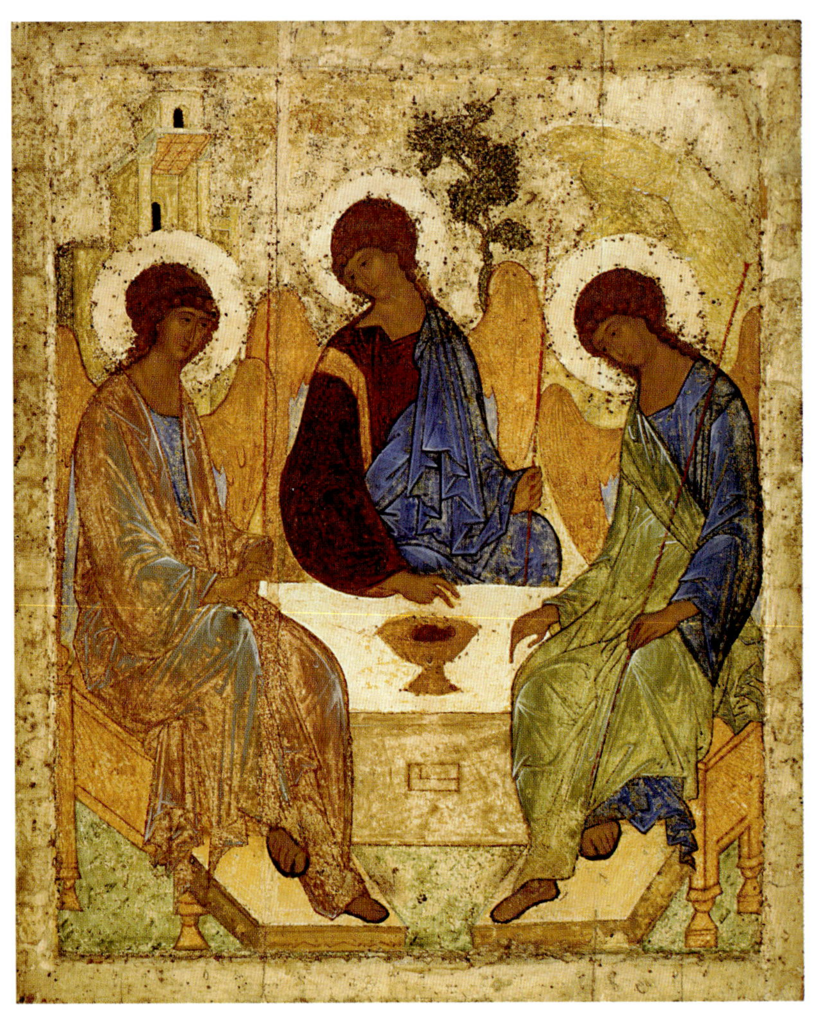

2 Rublev, *Old Testament Trinity*, 1420s, gesso and tempera on wood.

The Trinity

In recounting Rublev's life, it would be more than convenient if one could follow the king's advice to the White Rabbit in *Alice's Adventures in Wonderland*: begin at the beginning, go on to the end, and stop. This, as we have seen, cannot be done. We do not know the beginnings of Rublev's life or career; as for its end, in a broad sense no stopping point has yet been reached. Somewhere between these limits, however, we can locate Rublev's pivotal achievement: the painting of the *Old Testament Trinity* icon, without which he would be little more than a footnote to history (illus. 2).

So that is where we shall start our story. In the process, it should be possible to introduce some fundamental thoughts on icons: what, why and how they represented what they did. Icons are often thought of as static objects of veneration, generally showing stylized saintly or biblical figures; they can be so, but can also be dynamic, full of implicit movement. In the case of the Rublev *Old Testament Trinity* an icon can also be a memorial, in this instance – according to the seventeenth-century *Story of the Holy Icon Painters* – to St Sergius, standing as it did for centuries in the lowest tier of the first stone church of Sergius's own Trinity monastery (illus. 3). Simultaneously it can have didactic and philosophical purposes, illuminating Sergius's principle of the vanquishing of enmity through concord in diversity. The Trinity too has particular resonance as an iconographic subject, in that its precise nature was a major cause of dispute in the schism between Orthodoxy and Roman Catholicism.

Anyone who, given museum conditions, can get reasonably close to Rublev's *Old Testament Trinity* will witness a battle-scarred relic, or survivor. It consists of three boards of lime (that is, linden) wood – two of which had moved slightly apart, despite struts on the back, and had to be reunited in the twentieth century – together forming a large, near-square surface (114 × 142 cm – a ratio approximating to 1: root 2, often encountered in early buildings). The figurative paintwork is within a slight depression (*kovcheg*, or ark), as usual in Russian medieval icons. It became common to use the margins surrounding the *kovcheg* for further scenes, often narrative in nature, or inscriptions, but not here. There was an inscription, 'Holy Trinity', in red on the main paint surface, now almost illegible. The painted surface is in parts greatly worn, and has many little nail holes in some areas. Much of the robe of the left-hand figure is worn; so is the table, down to the original gesso (it is thought that there were triangular pieces of bread on it originally). The tree is in large part a repainting. The mouths of the figures may owe something to touching up (I have my suspicions about the distinctly Pre-Raphaelite look of the left-hand angel). Compared with the beautiful hands, the feet are rather clumpy. But most of the paintwork is fairly well preserved.

Almost filling the painted scene are three figures, richly clad, seated yet rather strangely so to the viewer, arranged around a plain table so as to form, in the readings of different commentators, a circular pattern (symbolic of eternity), a triangle, a hexagon, an octagon; interacting with one another rhythmically, though silently. They are unidentifiable as old or young, male or female (though beardless), and behind them are discreet wings, around their heads haloes, once gilded. They are, of course, angels. Well in the background, but seeming to grow out of the three figures themselves, are three objects: a simple if elegant pavilion or house,

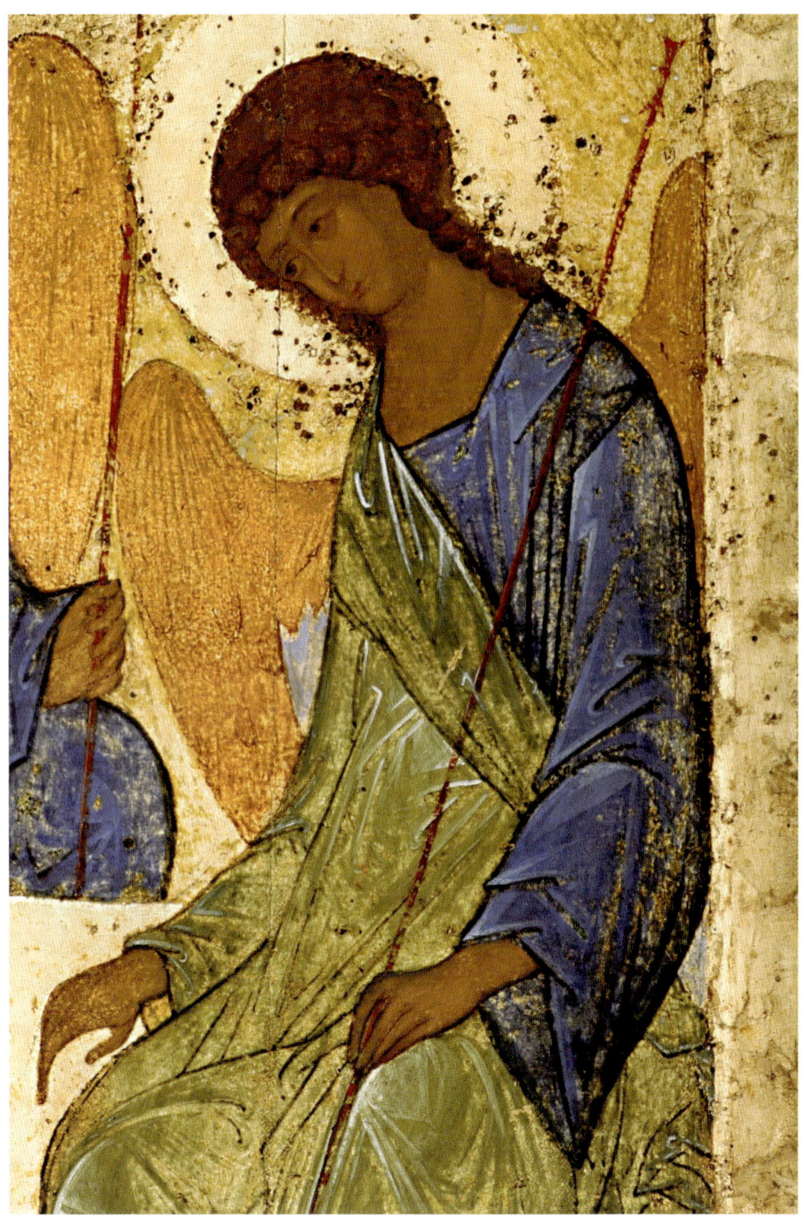

3 Rublev, *Old Testament Trinity*, detail of the right-hand figure in the
icon, generally held to represent the Holy Spirit – melding the worldliness
of green with the spirituality of deep blue.

a tree and a curving mountain top. The angelic figures are also travellers, as signified by the delicate staff each holds; the free hands of each variously gesticulate towards a chalice, imposed with no attempt at perspective on the table, containing a rather shocking splash of blood red (echoed in the sleeve of the central figure), and once holding a sacrificial calf's head.

At this point one may well mention the first thing that may strike the viewer about this picture: the astonishing colouration. Bold red and blue characterize the garments of the central angel: the blue, echoed in the other two figures, is no less than lapis lazuli, the rarest and most expensive of pigments. It hangs in rather well-defined folds. By contrast the deep red creeps like a bloodstain – though interrupted by a golden shoulder sash. Paler colours characterize the rest of the scene: the pinkish garment of the left-hand angel, the grass-green of that on the right. But all their wings are a pale gold, together making up a continuous backcloth. The bright scarlet so characteristic of Russian (particularly Novgorod) icons is absent. It has long been a critical commonplace to relate Rublev's colours to those of a Russian summer landscape.

What is being represented here? The Holy Trinity, as would be clear from the inscription; but the three persons of God (Father, Son and Holy Spirit) cannot be directly depicted in the Orthodox Church, since 'No man hath seen God at any time' (John 1:18, cf. too 6:46); though occasionally God the Father was shown as the 'Ancient of Days' (Daniel 7), a scheme rejected in the seventeenth century. Thus to show the Trinity pictorially, on an icon or a church wall, a symbolic representation is required, and for this the Orthodox Church has long chosen the somewhat puzzling episode in the story of Abraham where the Lord appears in the form of three men, whom he welcomes with a meal. As recounted in Genesis 18:1–8 (King James Bible), it reads:

And the LORD appeared to him in the plains of Mamre: and he sat in the tent door in the heat of the day; And he lift up his eyes and looked, and lo, three men stood by him; and when he saw them, he ran to meet them from the tent door, and bowed himself toward the ground. And said, My Lord, if I have found favour in thy sight, pass not away, I pray thee, from thy servant: Let a little water, I pray you, be fetched, and wash your feet, and wash yourself under the tree: And I will fetch a morsel of bread, and comfort ye your hearts; after that ye shall pass on: for therefore are ye come to your servant. And they said, So do, as thou hast said. And Abraham hastened into the tent unto Sarah, and said, Make ready quickly three measures of fine meal, knead it, and make cakes upon the hearth. And Abraham ran unto the herd, and fetcht a calf tender and good, and gave it unto a young man; and he hasted to dress it. And he took butter, and milk, and the calf which he had dressed, and set it before them; and he stood by them under the tree, and they did eat.

Thereupon the men summon Sarah and inform her and Abraham that, despite their great age, they will have a son: for 'Abraham shall surely become a great and mighty nation' (Genesis 18:18). Thereafter the Lord in the form of the three men departs to inspect Sodom and the sinful 'cities of the plain'. They are not specifically identified as angels (until two are, in the following chapter), but collectively they represent God, of whom angels are the messengers, and speak on his behalf.

This brief episode was meaningful beyond its apparent scope. The Old Testament is rooted in the story of Abraham; his predicted son, Isaac, will be taken to a mountain and nearly sacrificed as a test of his obedience to God's will. Old Testament events were taken to prefigure those in the New, and as we have

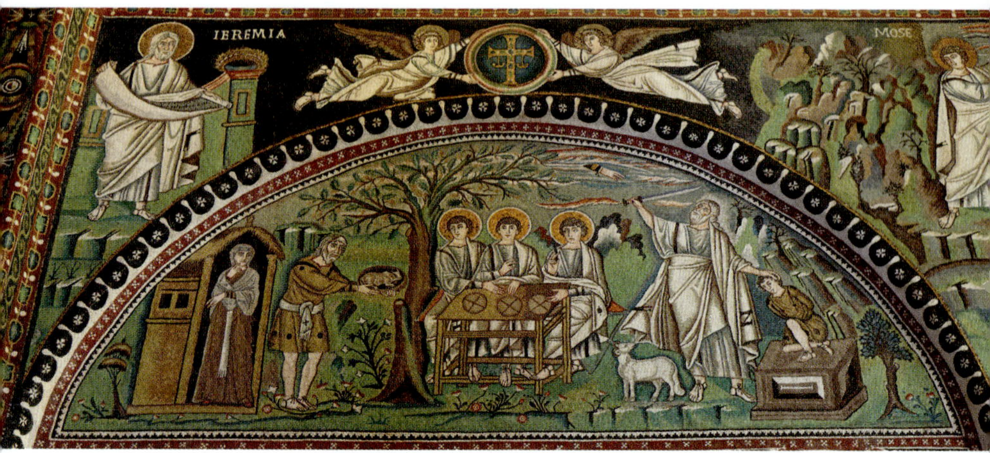

4 Hospitality of Abraham, Basilica of San Vitale, Ravenna, early
Byzantine glass mosaic panel, mid-6th century. The three angels are
seated side-by-side, undifferentiated, under the Oak of Mamre, with
Abraham and Sarah to the left, and a cross representing Christ above.
As part of the story of Abraham, it leads directly into the scene of the
Sacrifice of Isaac (right).

seen these three men or angels prefigure the Trinity. Beyond
them there remain just token reminders of significant objects:
the classical pavilion that is Abraham's 'tent'; the lone Oak
(Bunge suggests a terebinth) of Mamre, sacred tree; the most
unusually depicted mountain on which Isaac was about to be
sacrificed (or the stone upon which Jacob laid his head and
dreamed of a ladder to heaven: Genesis 28) – perhaps even, if
one dare enter the world of Russian folklore, it is the magical
white 'stone of stones', Alatyr (not as fantastical as it might
seem, since it had strong Christian references, though I have
never seen this idea put forward; the mysterious white stone of
Revelation 2:17 may also be relevant, as too the many biblical
references to the Lord as a 'rock', for example in Psalm 71).

    There are representations of the Hospitality going back to
early Christian times, and the three guests are normally placed
rather lamely side-by-side, with Abraham and Sarah busying

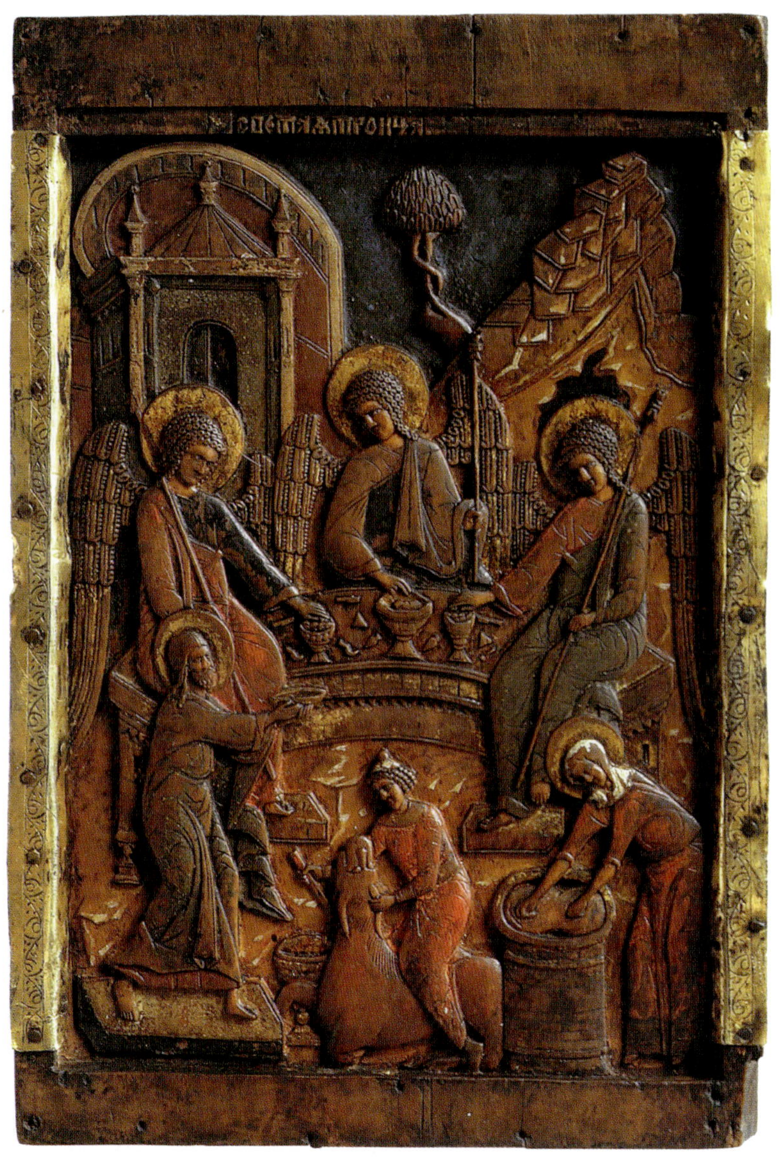

5 *Old Testament Trinity*, Vologda province, 16th century, carved wood
with egg tempera painting and silver-gilt bands. In the north, many
iconic objects were carved of wood, often further decorated, as here;
the treatment of the subject owes little to Rublev, dominated as it is
by scenes relating to the feast.

themselves and a substantial feast on the table, if not also a scene
of slaughter. Not only does this usually lead to a somewhat awk-
ward arrangement of the personnel involved, but it concentrates
on the narrative rather than the event's timeless significance.
Rublev could have got his idea to arrange the angels in a semi-
circle from small round pilgrims' badges or other tokens (illus. 6),
but his total omission of Abraham and Sarah in a large icon is a
remarkable tour de force. Icons following older patterns continued to be painted, but after Rublev's time nearly all paid
attention, at least, to his configuration (illus. 5). Sometimes painters wished to signal which of the angels represented which of the
Trinitarian persons, often putting a cross into the halo on the
Son, but this was a futile pursuit. For what it is worth, most

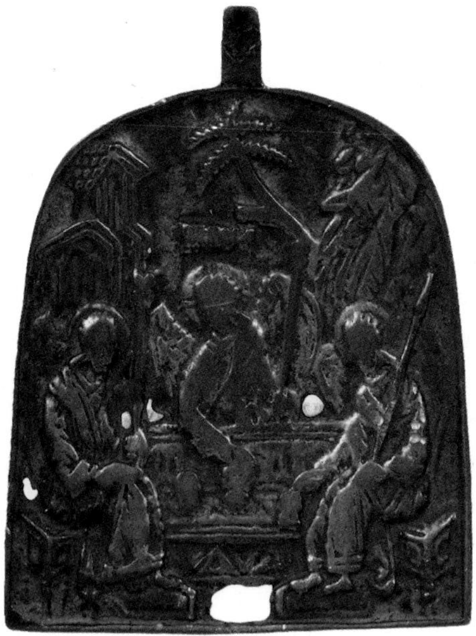

6 Miniature copper icon of the *Old Testament Trinity*, 15th century.
It was a popular subject for various round or nearly round badges,
pilgrim souvenirs, and Panagia medallions worn by bishops in the
East Christian world, thus perhaps suggesting to Rublev a circular
disposition of his figures in his own great icon.

commentators agree that the left-hand figure of Rublev's work is the Father, the right-hand one the Holy Spirit, but this diminishes their unity – though he subtly differentiates between them through gesture and expression, and the central figure's hand pointing to the chalice, signifying suffering, is surely unambiguous. Doubtless the figures' multivalency was also the painter's way of expressing the message of the Epistle to the Hebrews (13:2): 'Be not forgetful to entertain strangers: for thereby some have entertained angels unawares.' But picturing angels was hardly a straightforward matter: earlier such representations had been, to put it crudely, too human or too bird-like. 'To depict angels at all was complicated, because they were thought to be incorporeal . . . they were technically silent as well.'[2] Yet their song fills the church building when the congregation gives voice. The rhythmic qualities of the *Trinity* icon, which so many commentators have noted, surely have to be a symbol of this unheard musicality, while the three figures are evidently in silent mutual converse. Rublev's solution to the problem of 'angelic representation' is a major feat, one that shows the potential open-endedness of the iconic world. In this connection, one is reminded of the mystic philosopher P. Ouspensky, writing in 1912 that 'Wishing to understand the noumenal world, we must seek a hidden meaning in everything' accessible to the artist alone: 'an artist must be a clairvoyant, he must see that which others do not see. And he must be a magician, must possess the gift of making others see what they do not see by themselves.'[3]

Rublev was surely one such magician. The aura of his *Trinity* lives on; it has even made it on to postage stamps, and into a much-appreciated sculpture standing in the city centre of Yaroslavl. We are used to literary texts being subject to a variety of approaches and interpretations, some more plausible than others; there is no reason why this should not equally apply to a major work of art.

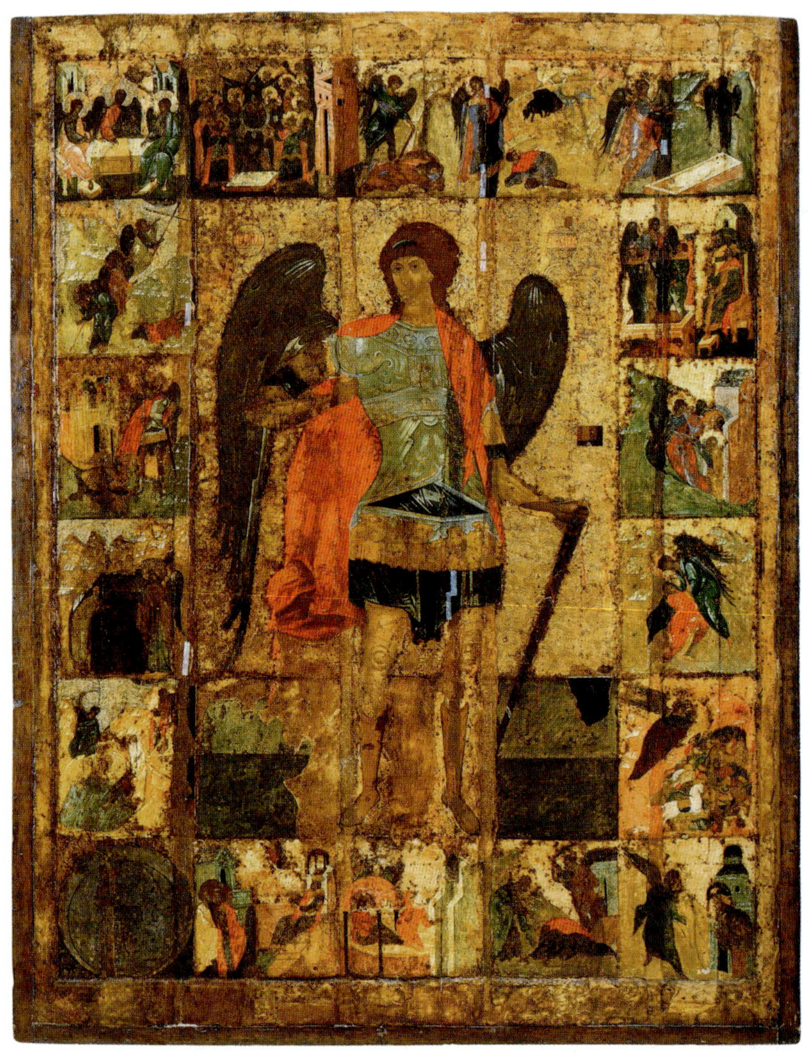

7 Archangel Michael as warrior saint, with marginal scenes (top left, a Trinity), *c.* 1399, attributed to Feofan Grek and his team, now in Archangel Cathedral of Moscow Kremlin; note the remarkable contrast with the Zvenigorod St Michael.

TWO

Russia, *c.* 1400: Being Russian, Being a Monk, Being a Painter

'These are the narratives of bygone years regarding the origin of the land of Rus, who first began to rule in Kiev, and from what source the land of Rus had its beginning.' So starts the Russian Primary Chronicle (*c.* 1110), from which 'source' all subsequent accounts of Russian history (and there were many), up to the eighteenth century, had their beginning. Russia has a long history, during much of which it has worried about its own identity, and to put Rublev's lifetime into context we have to go far back into it. In the first millennium of our era Slav tribes infiltrated the lands of what are now Russia, Ukraine and Belarus, then thinly populated by Finno-Ugrian, subsequently Baltic, hunter-gatherers. Viking or 'Varangian' traders followed – apparently the first to be known as 'Rus', or 'oarsmen' – seeking routes to Constantinople and the East.

As the Primary Chronicle has it, in 862 the Varangians, having first been expelled by the Slavs, were invited back to rule, since 'our land is rich, but has no order in it.' So began the dynasty of the legendary Ryurik and his offspring; they were certainly long-lasting, since their successors ruled the Russian lands not only in Rublev's lifetime but for nearly two hundred more years. Soon settling down with the locals and intermarrying not only with them, but into most of the royal houses of Europe, they founded a powerful and successful state, with princes from the dynasty installed in the main towns of a dozen or so tribal bases, ready to relocate over the vast territory of Rus when the death or deposition of the main ruler, enthroned in the strategically placed city of Kiev, demanded it.

Princes had a retinue (*druzhina*, the same word as later used for a team of painters), who were to form the basis of the land-owning class; otherwise, there were no orders of chivalry or proper feudalism. In the absence of a fixed law of primogeniture the system was built on shaky foundations. As generations passed, the desire to put down local roots increased, as did internecine rivalries between princes, of which steppe-based marauders could and did take full advantage; also the division and subdivision of large principalities into appanages for the younger members of a given family.

Andrey Rublev's activity unrolled in what, less than a century before, had seemed a small and quite unremarkable appanage – Moscow – awarded earlier to the youngest son of the warrior-prince Alexander 'Nevsky'. Before we discuss it, we need to consider three fundamental events in early Russian history. In 988/9, the prince of Kiev, Vladimir I, ceremoniously orchestrated the most famous of them – the conversion to Christianity, on the Byzantine model. We hardly need to spell out the consequences: not only the imposition of a new belief system (though there had been Christians in Kiev before) but the transplantation of a whole cultural package deal. The next key moment took place in 1169, when the prince of Vladimir, Andrey Bogolyubsky ('Beloved of God'), recipient of the Kievan throne, not only refused to move but sent a force to rout the city. Thereafter Kiev never regained its former significance, and the centre of gravity of Rus shifted to the northeast. This was not a sudden process, as Franklin and Shepard make clear, but it was irreversible. The third moment came in 1237–40, when the Mongol – in Russia, always known as 'Tatar' – armies of Chingiz (or Genghis) Khan picked off the cities of Rus one by one (though not Novgorod), finishing by sacking Kiev and placing the whole country under tribute. Tatar *baskaki*, enforcers, were installed in the main towns, and princes had to be confirmed in office at the Tatar headquarters – in particular 'Grand Princes', entrusted with tax-gathering, some of whom did not escape with their lives.

Medieval Rus was an agricultural country, as was most of Europe, but that did not mean that towns were unimportant – they were marketplaces, gathering-places for trade (a very important element of Russian viability), centres of craft production. There were several levels of society, their status and obligations not well understood today, including bondsmen, but it seems the majority were free peasants, able to change employment around the second St George's Day, in November. Though early Rus knew plenty of military skirmishing, the Tatar assault was on a different level: systematically destroying cities, impressing many craftsmen into Tatar service, killing indiscriminately. Having an army was counterproductive for a city: Alexander Nevsky, no slouch at heroic resistance, wisely persuaded his fellow Novgorodians to pay up and be spared. Alexander's youngest son, Daniil, founded the line of princes who, inheriting the insignificant appanage of Moscow, bit by bit enlarged it through fair means or foul with remarkable single-mindedness. Naturally, as appanages got smaller and poorer, they became all the more liable to be purchased or simply swallowed up by expansionist neighbours.

As was bound to happen, the situation with regard to the Tatars changed as the decades after the first onslaught passed. What had seemed like an unimaginable natural disaster settled into a merely annoying pattern of existence (that is, until a Tatar force decided to ravage the Russian countryside, usually as a punishment for late payment). The Tatar realm itself was prone to division, and Rus came under the aegis of the Golden Horde, centred on the Volga. *Baskaki* were withdrawn, so the system was self-policing. It was advantageous to be confirmed as Grand

Prince – responsible for delivering tax revenue – and Moscow jostled for this through the first half of the fourteenth century with its nearby rival Tver, well situated on the upper Volga, but without much of a productive hinterland.

Moscow ultimately played its cards more cannily than Tver (which lost several princes at the Horde). From the reign of Ivan I Kalita ('Moneybags', d. 1341), there were several decades of relative peace, notwithstanding the assaults of the Black Death – less of a menace in the countryside than in cities – during which Rublev was born and grew up. Dmitriy Ivanovich (r. 1359–89) tested the by now fragmented Tatars in various ways, culminating in the great set-piece battle of Kulikovo. His reign and that of his son, Vasiliy I (r. 1389–1425), witnessed considerable building activity and a general cultural revival. It was overly optimistic to imagine the 'Tatar yoke' as coming to an immediate end, yet the almost casual way in which Dmitriy's will mentions the possibility, amid the lengthy parcelling out among his children of the villages, apiaries, knick-knacks and so on that constituted his patrimony, shows that Tatar rule had become an irritant rather than a major national humiliation ('And if God brings about a change regarding the Horde, and my children do not have to give Tatar tribute, then the tribute that each of my sons collects in his patrimonial principality shall be his' – in other words, pocket the cash and count yourself lucky). Dmitriy, like Rublev, was canonized in 1988.

Where in all this stood the Russian Church? It remained of course an all-Russian institution, headed by the Metropolitan of Kiev and All Rus (as he remained until the mid-fifteenth century). In an age of fragmentation and foreign occupation, with international links all but severed, its very existence served to remind people of who they were and to keep a permanent line of communication open with Constantinople and the East Christian world. Kiev itself had been comprehensively wrecked and almost depopulated (as testified by the Papal Legate, Friar John of Plano Carpini, who passed through on his way to the Great Horde), and eventually, circa 1299, the Metropolitan relocated to Vladimir, where the great twelfth-century Cathedral of the Dormition (that is, the Assumption) still stood. In the late 1320s Metropolitan Peter moved further, to Moscow, then ruled by the wise Ivan Kalita, though Moscow rulers still went to Vladimir to be enthroned – and the main Vladimir relics, notably the twelfth-century 'Virgin of Vladimir' icon, made occasional 'visits' to Moscow (these visits seem to have been commemorated by the making of copies of the icon).

The linking of the Moscow principality with the central authority of the Church was a major boost to the reputation of the former, particularly under the notable, and later canonized, Metropolitan Aleksey (d. 1378), founder of the Andronikov Monastery of the Saviour among others, effective ruler of the country during the childhood of Dmitriy Donskoy. The onslaught of the 'pagan' Tatars (who soon converted to Islam) galvanized ordinary Russians to determine and proclaim their own identity, henceforth resolutely Christian (of which the word for peasant, *khrestianin*, is a variant).

The slow process of Christianization had by then reached all recesses of the countryside – which of course certainly did not mean that all pre-Christian folk beliefs or practices had irrevocably died out. Rather, they had become 'desemanticized', their origins lost. Quite frequently Orthodox clerics inveighed against such lax and apparently un-Christian goings-on, without apparently having much permanent effect. An early example, known as the 'Sermon of a certain Christlover', was discovered in 1847 in a miscellany dating from the fourteenth to fifteenth centuries, and refers to people living 'double-believingly' – which allowed nineteenth- and twentieth-century historians to speculate on the existence of popular 'double belief': simultaneous adherence to two belief systems, a pagan and a Christian one. Modern scholarship has seriously undermined this interpretation.[4]

In Tarkovsky's film *Andrei Rublev*, there is an interesting spin-off from these questions. Its central episode, named in the film 'The Holiday', is set on St John the Baptist's Eve (23 June) 1408. A large group of naked pagans are lighting bonfires and swimming. Such goings-on, and more besides, have characterized that important day – reckoned then to be the solstice – into modern times; they seem to derive from fertility rituals. Yet the participants can hardly be real pagans, nor is it likely that Andrey would have been ignorant of these practices. Equally the scene where an itinerant jester (*skomorokh*) is beaten up might more fittingly belong to the seventeenth century, when the state made a serious effort to clamp down on such entertainers, rather than to Rublev's time.

The Tatars had a treat up their sleeve for the Russian church: in the early fourteenth century they issued proclamations freeing the Church from all tax burdens, allowing it to control itself and administer its own laws (as elsewhere in Christendom, much of the justice system was under Church jurisdiction). This helped to relieve the overall weight of taxes on society and encouraged the growth of Church property – if you have money to bequeath or donate, why not take advantage of a tax break, and be prayed for, too? – but it did not in the long run prevent churches and monasteries suffering from devastation in events like the sack of Vladimir, or the torching of whole villages, church-owned or not, in subsequent Tatar attacks. A monastery, with its solid wooden walls, could be safer than a village, which would have had nothing mroe than a fence; indeed, when stone or brick generally replaced wood in the sixteenth century, the larger monasteries resembled fortresses, and by the seventeenth century – particularly in the 'Time of Troubles' – became such. Monastic life arrived, of course, as part of the East Christian package at the Conversion. Its origins are the same as in Western Christendom, but it developed somewhat differently: instead of individual monastic orders, each with its own rules and purposes, Eastern monasticism continued to maintain a simpler and older form.

Individual hermits, who would establish their own pattern of life and prayer, might join up in a small community known as a skete (from the Scetis valley in Egypt), with individual cells meeting for communal worship on appropriate occasions – an idiorrhythmic existence now found in larger monasteries only on Mount Athos. Any sizeable group implied a coenobitic institution, with an abbot, more or less strict rules and a communal life (which is the meaning of the word). Large monasteries provided welfare and hospitals for the poor. Such were the institutions into which Russian hermitages developed, with sketes as a halfway house. New arrivals would remain as novices, maybe for years (they had to learn the text of the Psalms by heart), before being admitted to the brotherhood, changing their names, and donning the black hood or *klobuk*, indicating status as a warrior against evil – hence the term *chernets*, 'black one', by which Rublev is described in the 1405 Trinity Chronicle.

A monk had relative security, purpose and work, and at least minimal food, in a classless community where he might be elevated from peasant toil; it was from the monastic ranks that Orthodox bishops were drawn (parish priests had to be married). Monasteries – not just in towns (like the Moscow Chudov and Simonov Monasteries), but some deep in the country (the Kirillov Monastery; the Trinity itself) – were also repositories of knowledge, in the absence of universities. Manuscripts were kept, copied and decorated there; some were major centres of chronicle composition. Their leading figures might be compelling and authoritative leaders and teachers.

What the monk had to give up was the contentment and indulgences of family life; a life of prayer and toil involved fasts for around half the year, and unquestioning obedience to the abbot and senior monks. We cannot of course know what motivated an individual to adopt this life, particularly where knowledge of his/her family background is entirely absent. Whatever motives Rublev might have had, they were certainly not those of career advancement. He probably joined a team and learned his artistic skills before entering the novitiate in the 1380s–90s. So far as we can judge from chronicles, nearly all fourteenth-century painters in Moscow, and most of those thereafter, were laymen. They could be well rewarded, whereas a monk would not profit personally (his monastery might do, of course). In Rublev's case, one can well envisage him as having been a seeker after knowledge, keen to make use of the spiritual and intellectual resources that the Trinity and Andronikov monasteries could abundantly provide. Both Joseph of Volokolamsk and Pakhomy refer to Rublev's 'thoughtfulness', his quality of productive contemplation.

Learning to be a painter was a slow business, particularly where it involved wall painting. It took boldness, good organization and considerable outlay to take charge of such an operation – something anyhow unknown in Moscow until its first stone church was built to contain the remains of the Metropolitan Peter in the late 1320s. Wooden scaffolding would be needed. Pigments would be assembled in broad wooden bowls: no problem for earth colours (ochres, in general), expensive when it came to brilliant blues (lapis lazuli, azurite) or reds (cinnabar, sinopia). These would be suspended in lime water and applied while the wall plaster was wet. Teams worked very quickly; often a chronicle would record 'they finished in the same year' – only in the summer season could such work be done. On my first visit to Ferapontov Monastery, in mid-May 1990, I was surprised to find the church full of wooden scaffolding. 'Is it still under restoration?' I asked. 'Oh no, the wood is to soak up people's breath, which would

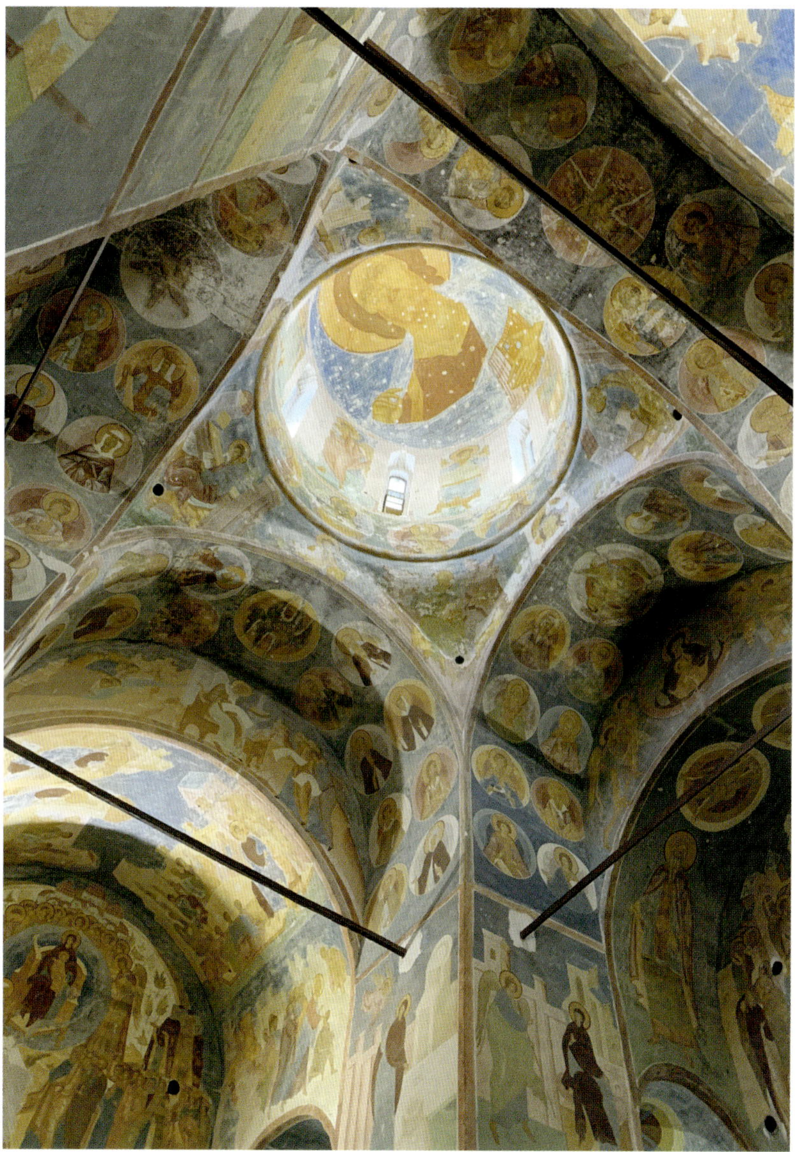

8 Interior view of the Ferapontov Monastery Cathedral. This monastery, near Kirillov, was founded in 1480, and fully painted by Dionisiy and his two sons in 1502 (as recorded in an inscription). The paintings almost all survive and depict (among much else) hymns to the Mother of God; it is often considered that they mark the end of the 'Age of Rublev'.

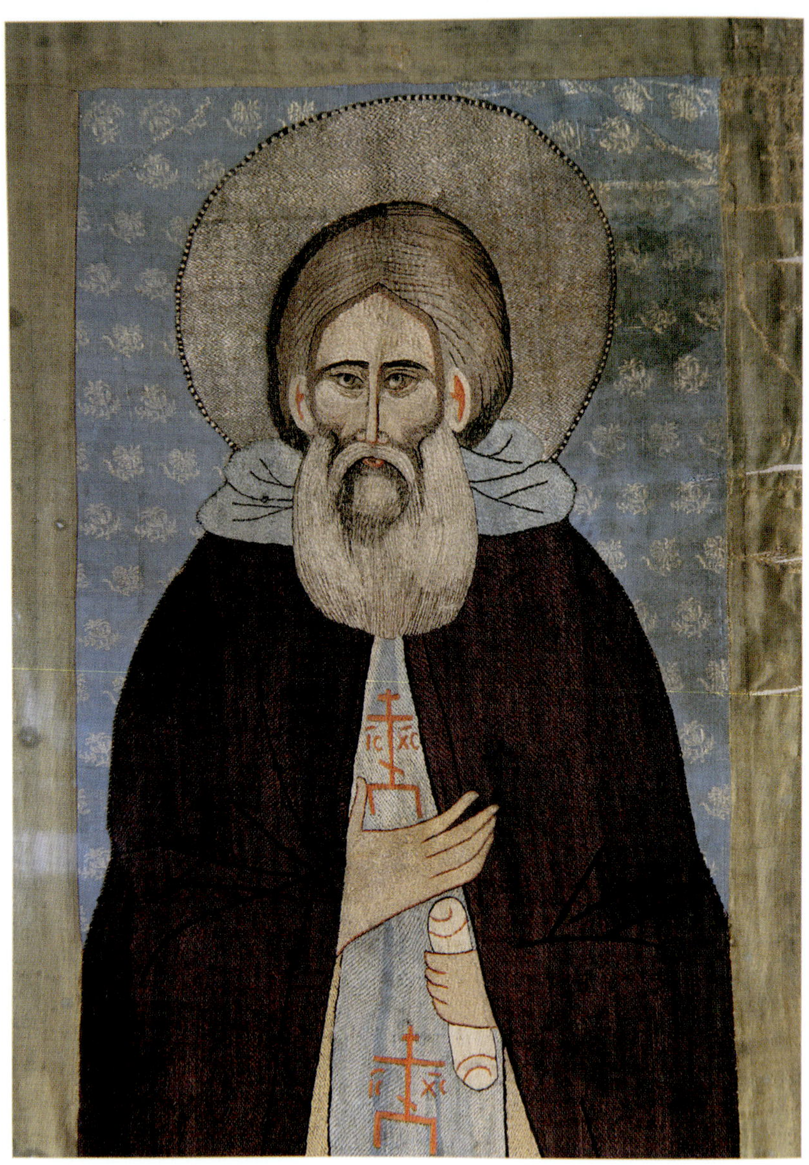

9 St Sergius embroidery, *c.* 1422. Fine cloths such as shrouds, palls, altar cloths, vestments, various hangings and so on – all the work of craftswomen, often using costly imported materials and silk thread – are characteristic of the 15th century.

condense on the walls,' I was told – it had only recently been opened after winter, and had not yet warmed up. A proud inscription on its north wall records that it was apparently painted between 6 August and 8 September 1502, by Dionisiy and his two sons – an astonishing feat of organization, even if Dionisiy's manner, though many-figured, tends to dispense with the elegant detail found in Rublev's and Daniil's wall painting in Vladimir. Specialists have indeed identified 34 giornate – day-stages – in the body of the cathedral (illus. 8). This was religious painting,

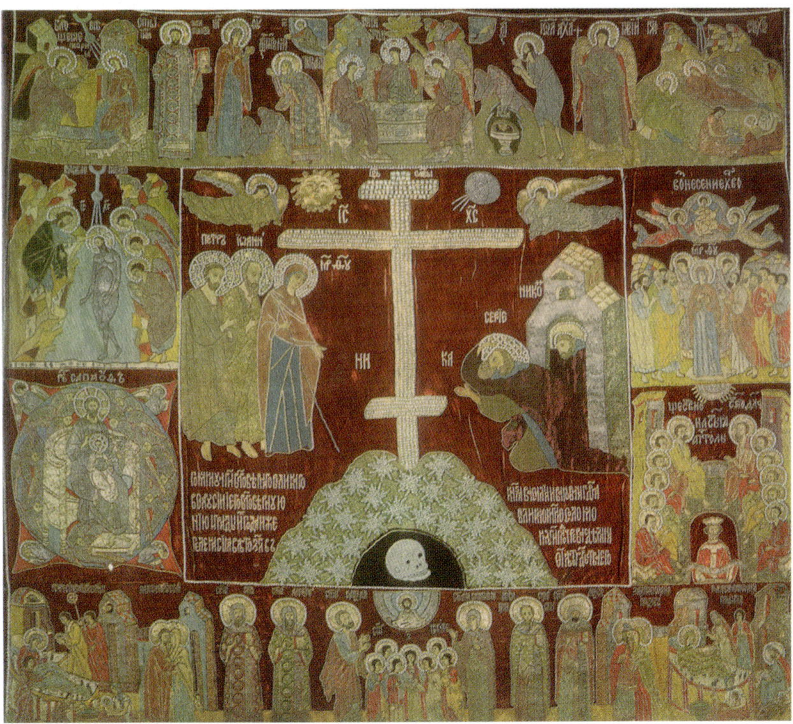

10 'The Mother of God Appears to Sergius', 1525, a splendid embroidery made at the behest of Vasiliy III and his wife, anxious for a son, and presented to the Trinity Monastery; it is believed to have been designed by one of Dionisiy's sons. Silk, gold and silver thread, with pearls, are used. Note Rublev's 'Trinity' scheme above, and on the left so-called 'Paternity' – a way of representing Father, Son and Holy Spirit.

at which the experts would have long been skilled. But what of the palace paintings that, as we learn from Yepifany, Feofan Grek undertook in Moscow – one of them 'an extraordinary and wondrous scene'? We can do no more than guess.

As for icon painting, both prospects and skills were rather different. There was presumably a steady demand for icons, though we cannot know how widely distributed they would have been in people's houses at that stage. The preparation of an icon took knowhow. A board of suitable wood had to be cut and prepared, with a depression on the surface and slits cut at the back for strengthening dowels (which tended in fact to be ineffective). A piece of loose woven cloth would be attached to the surface with fish glue. Several ever-finer layers of gesso would cover the surface; then, after polishing, maybe with such a plant as mare's tail, painting could begin, building up from dark colours to light. If gold leaf was applied, say on haloes, it would be glued in place with cut garlic. Egg yolk would be the usual medium of suspension for pigments – which themselves needed preparation. Small scenes of the major incidents of saints' lives were commonly placed in the borders, though no surviving icons attributable to Rublev or his team show these (illus. 7).

With this activity, maybe book copying and skilled metal-work too, the five- or six-month-long winter could be filled. In this connection one should mention that pictorial art embraced more than panel icons: there are many fine early medieval embroi-deries (the artistic sphere of craftswomen) surviving, among which one may single out the grandest of all, made in Rublev's lifetime: the 'Great Sakkos' (liturgical robe) of the Metropolitan Photios (1408–31), embroidered with pearls, over fifty individ-ual scenes and texts mostly in Greek but also in Slavonic. Later, fine embroideries featuring Sergius himself would be made (illus. 9, 10).

THREE

The World of Rublev:
From Makovets to Maura

Rublev's life span (c. 1360s–1430) coincides with a pivotal time in Russian history, though this is seldom understood by non-Russians, or even by Russians themselves, who may tend to think of the whole long period from 1240 until 1480 as simply that of the 'Tatar yoke'. As a curiosity, one may note that it comes at the exact midpoint through the Russian historical record: from the invitation to the Vikings to 'come and rule us' (862) to our time of publication (2022). It was also, as we have seen, a period when Moscow was cementing its position as leader among the various Russian principalities, though this was slow to become apparent. More dramatically, it witnessed the beginning of the northward push of the Trans-Volga Elders, who, inspired by Sergius, founded well over a hundred ever more distant hermitages – many of which grew into monasteries – in ever further places in the northlands (such elders were so called since here the upper Volga flows west to east; north of it, the land was then relatively little inhabited).

This is a simple narrative and not necessarily incorrect, but there are further nuances and complications. Varfolomey, the future Sergius, was the second son of wealthy boyars from Rostov, dispossessed and impoverished when Moscow sacked and took over Rostov in 1327. His family moved to Radonezh, a small appanage town just inside the Moscow borders; thence (dates are uncertain), after their parents had died, Sergius and his

brother Stefan founded a hermitage themselves on a deeply
forested hilltop known as Makovets (a word related to 'summit'),
a short way northeast of Radonezh.

At this point a word of caution is needed. What we know
about Sergius depends on Yepifaniy's 'Life' (compiled from notes
he made over the course of twenty years from Sergius's death in
1392, he tells us). But of the seven medieval redactions of the
'Life' that survive – some longer, some shorter, some contained in
chronicles – none represents Yepifaniy's original text. As V. P.
Zubov skilfully demonstrated in 1953, all are to some extent the
product of Pakhomiy's rewritings in mid-century, often with
political considerations in mind. Such are the problems of text-
ology. The 'Life' of St Stephen of Perm (d. 1396), by contrast,

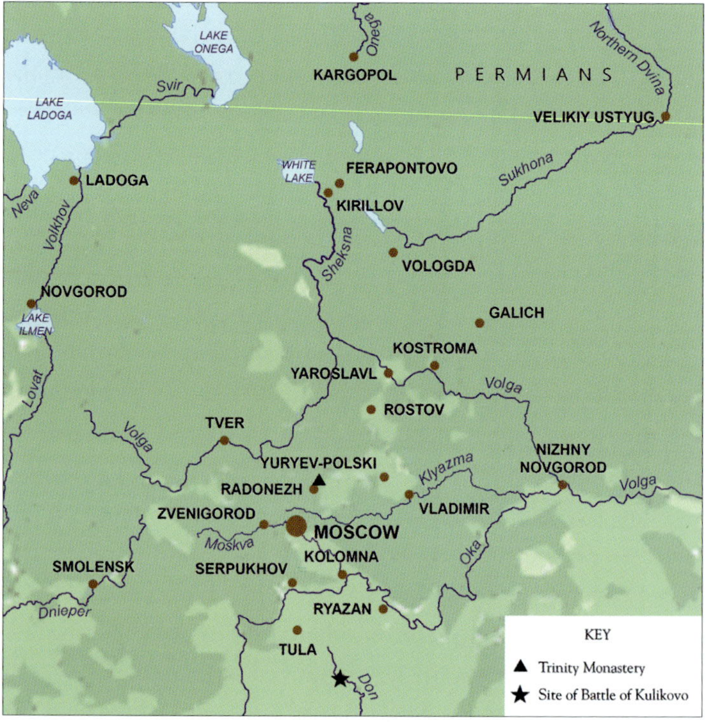

11 Middle Russia, approximately from Kargopol to Kulikovo Field.

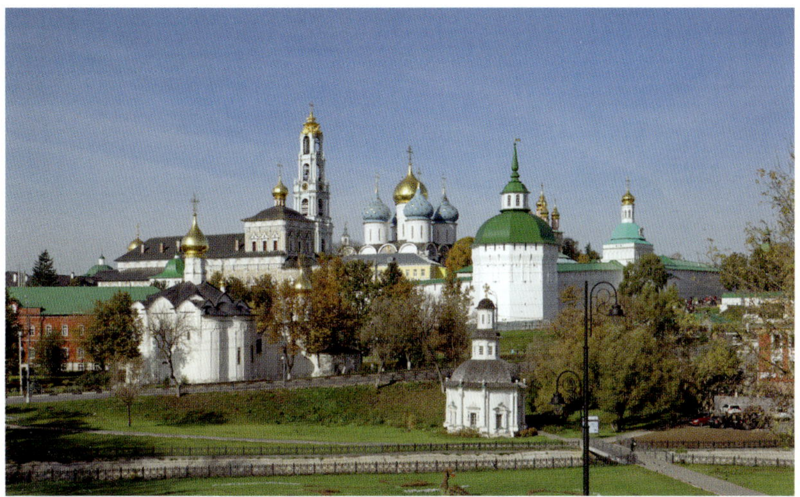

12 Trinity Monastery, present appearance, its mid-18th-century bell tower rising from the summit of the Hill of Makovets.

appears uncontaminated by later editing; we shall say more on him below.

The landscape to the north of Moscow is by no means flat, though rather unproductive (with much *podzol*, leached sandy soil with underlying hardpan, tending to swampiness and hard to till). It is traversed from southwest to northeast by an irregular line of moraine hills known nowadays as the Klin-Dmitrov Ridge. Within the ridge are fertile pockets, though mostly it is thickly forested. Stefan became a monk and joined a monastery in Moscow; Varfolomey established himself as a hermit on the hill of Makovets. Others joined Varfolomey, who took the name Sergius as a monk, and in the mid-1350s there was a fully fledged monastery, dedicated to the Holy Trinity, on this hill (illus. 12). Sergius came to be regarded as more than just a hermit – more a moral arbiter of fractured Russia (he turned down the offer to become Metropolitan of the Church). The monastery itself became a centre not just of spiritual strivings, but of learning: I have elsewhere argued that for a short time its growth seemed to promise an all-Russian focus capable of overcoming fractious divisions, and that in cultural history this is the 'Sergievan period'.[5]

The Black Death was meanwhile already sweeping through the Russian cities: was this not a factor encouraging escape to the countryside? Tatar raids were unpredictable, torching wooden towns and villages. There was every reason not just to move to Sergius's hermitage but to strike out further, to form hermitages in little-populated places by rivers and lakes ever further northwards. Living was hard, but away from the authorities and the tax-gatherers (whose proceeds still went to the Tatars) it was self-sufficient; monks survived by agricultural labour, and the extreme feats of self-mortification sometimes recorded elsewhere are unknown. The movement gained extraordinary momentum: by 1397 Sergius's disciple Kirill had reached what has become the town of Kirillov in the Land of the White Lake, Belozerye, a good 400 kilometres north of Sergiev Posad, as it became known (illus. 13). It was most easily reached by the Sheksna, a tributary of the Volga flowing from the north. Nowadays the canal from Moscow to St Petersburg largely follows the same course. As one gradually approaches the landing place at Goritsy, a distant pyramid appears on the skyline. This is the Hill of Maura, as momentous for the north as Makovets was for middle Russia, the steep-sided end of another moraine ridge. The road to Kirillov climbs up it, and from the top a splendid view unfolds.

It was here, according to his 'Life', that Kirill of the White Lake came with one companion, Ferapont, and beheld the forests, glades and lakes stretching out below. He decided to stay in this solitary though difficult place, planting a cross on a hillock beside Siverskaya lake. Ferapont, however, seeking somewhere more 'spacious' and 'smoother', left Kirill and moved 20 kilometres away, to a site overlooking Lake Borodava. His Ferapontov monastery stands there as a smaller pendant to

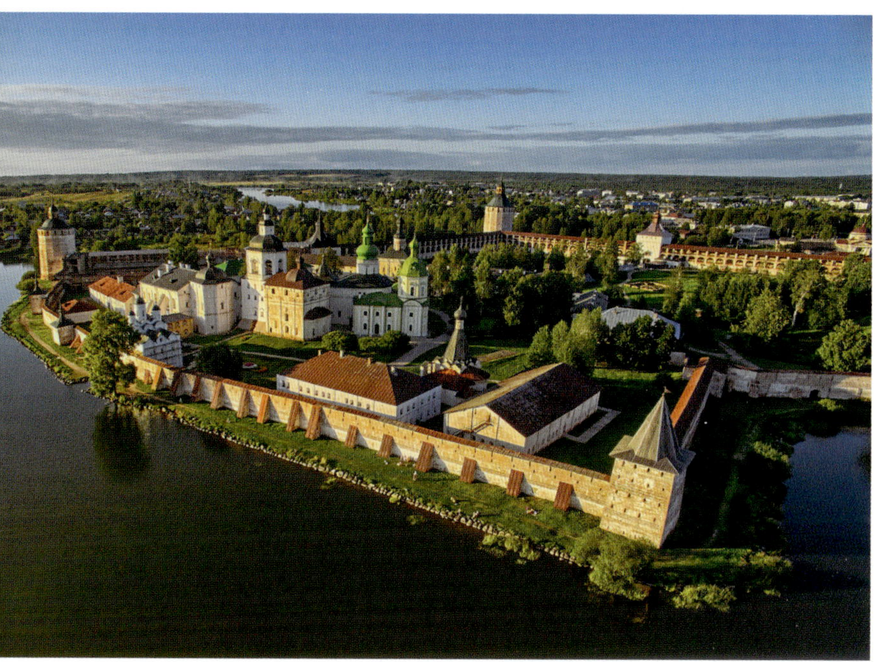

13 Kirillov Monastery 'of the White Lake', fronting Lake Siverskoye in a watery northern landscape.

the subsequently large Kirillov, which soon attracted monks and peasant settlers. They wanted a proper church, and a team of woodcutters conveniently turned up to provide one.

So goes the story. But it leaves questions. Kirill himself had left the Moscow Simonov Monastery abruptly after many years as abbot. For the Moscow authorities, it was useful, to say the least, to establish an outpost in far Belozerye, a sprawling territory abutting Novgorod's historic lands but conveniently close to land routes and waterways northwards. It was not quite so lonely as the 'Life' made out: there was a scattering of peasant settlers, not all of whom were well disposed to the incomers (and one of whom tried to set fire to their new settlement). Kirill himself – he lived to the age of ninety – was a notable disciplinarian and brought in a strict coenobitic rule for his brethren.

It is no surprise then that Ferapont departed soon afterwards to found his relatively small, though still coenobitic, commune. In the last year of Rublev's life, two further monks from Kirill's stable had reached the White Sea, twice as far from Kirillov as the latter was from the Trinity Monastery, and established what would become the major monastery on the archipelago of Solovki (then still in Novgorod territory).

Even more enterprising was the feat of Sergius's friend Stephen of Perm. He was born at Ustyug, where the lands of Novgorod adjoined those of the Permians (also known as the Zyrians, nowadays the Komi), a Finno-Ugric people. Stephen devised an alphabet and written language for them, translated sacred works into the Permian language and became their bishop (illus. 14). Alas, the Permian land was subsequently swallowed up by Muscovy. The 'Life' of Stephen (written before he was canonized), by Yepifaniy the Wise, was probably the best literary work of the age. Since Yepifany's name crops up more than once in these pages, and he is hardly a household name even in Russia (where the medieval language is no simpler to read than Middle English would be here), it may be worthwhile briefly characterizing this unusual work. A good hundred pages long, it intersperses the factual narrative of Stephen's doings with highly wrought passages displaying not only a hypnotic rhythmic facility, but all the devices of traditional rhetoric, and more

14 'Zyrian Trinity', icon of *Old Testament Trinity*, late 14th century. This remarkable painting must date from the time of St Stephen's mission to the Permian people, thus pre-dating Rublev, taking (and distorting) the ancient pattern of Abraham's three visitors seated side-by-side beneath a vast stylized tree, beside Abraham's tent – like a multi-storey palace. The pigments are rather dim earth colours. But its unique feature is a biblical inscription beneath the image of the angels, recounting the relevant story in the Permian language, using the script Stephen invented. It was discovered at the Trinity church of a village near Yarensk, at the edge of Permian (now Komi) territory.

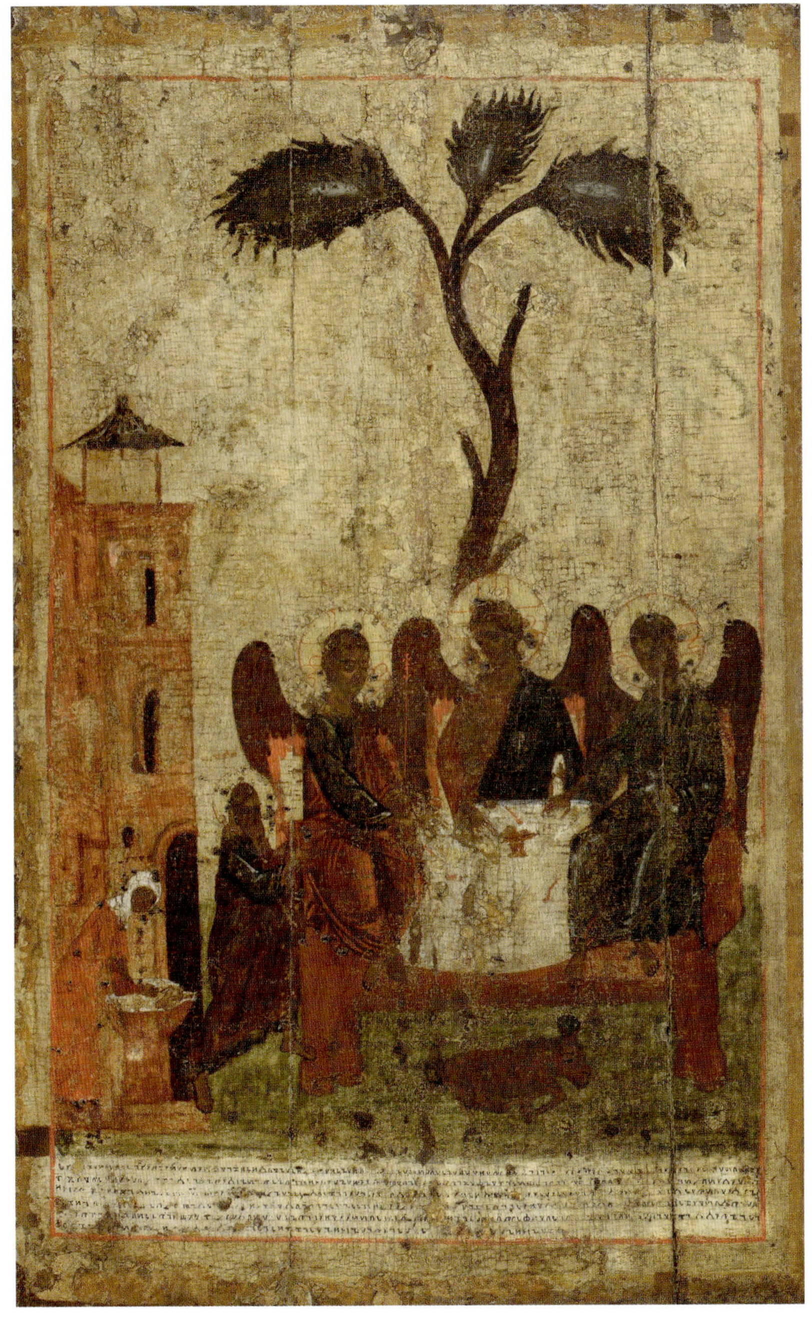

too – alliteration, internal rhymes, invented words – in a poetic self-devised linguistic register he himself terms 'word-weaving'.

The work is carefully structured: at its centre is a 'debate' with the chief Permian sorcerer (who is given colloquial Russian to speak, and who articulates a distinctly anti-Muscovite viewpoint). It ends with a poeticized, threefold set of laments: of the Permian people (that is, children for a father), of the Permian

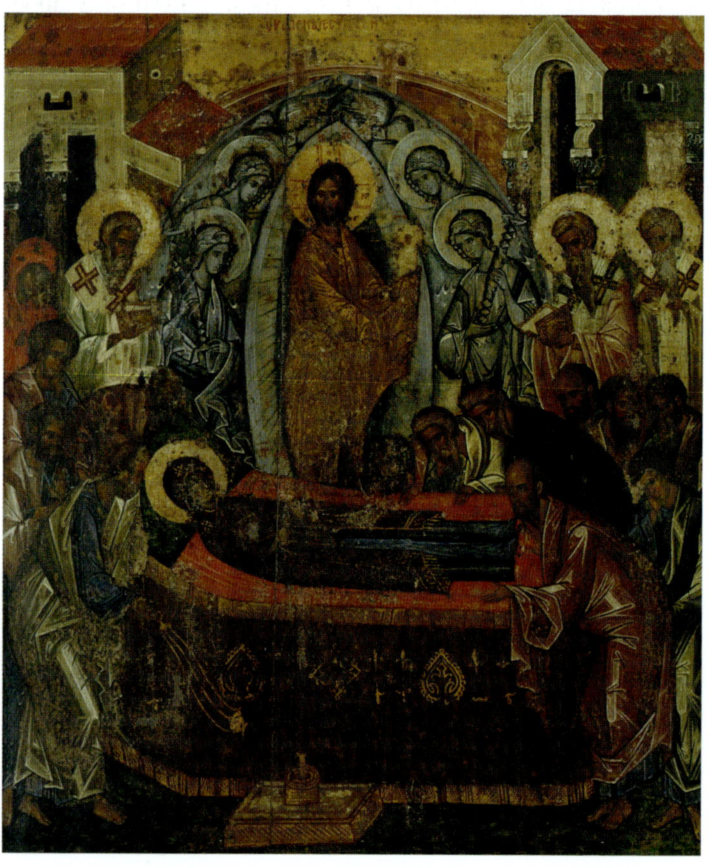

15 *Icon of the Dormition*, 15th century. This superb icon from the Kirillov Monastery – crowded with figures from the Heavenly Host, richly coloured and with virtuoso semi-transparent planes – stands in remarkable contrast to the earlier stark rendering by Feofan or one of his followers (see illus. 35).

church (a widow for a husband) and of the writer himself – a remarkable twist. The whole work is deliberately emotionalized, to the despair of nineteenth-century historians, though modern specialists, at least since the scholarly work of Dmitriy Likhachov, have come to appreciate it. The same devices are found in Yepifaniy's other 'Life', of Sergius, but re-editing of all its extant versions partially deprives us of its original verve and messages. It is notable that Yepifaniy seems to have written only about people he personally knew – these two 'Lives', and the letter about Feofan the Greek – probably in the hope of getting Sergius and Stephen canonized.

How does all this relate to Rublev's biography? These places may seem far away from his places of residence, yet are a close-knit network dependent on Sergius's vision and authority. There is no evidence Rublev ever went so far north, nor (in the absence of stone churches) would there have been a commission for him to do wall paintings there. But there are some magnificent fourteenth- and fifteenth-century icons at Kirillov, which soon established itself as a centre of learning and art. One, of the Dormition, has often on stylistic grounds been attributed to Rublev or his pupils (illus. 15), while the earliest known portrait of a living person in all Russian art, by Dionisiy Glushitsky (1362–1437), memorably showing an elderly Kirill, stood in a small niche with an inscription giving its date as 1424 (illus. 16). At Ferapontovo the late fifteenth-century cathedral contains an almost complete set of frescoes by Dionisiy and his sons, illustrative of hymns to the Mother of God, completed (as a long inscription records) in 1502 (see illus. 8). This is really the end of the 'Rublev century' of Russian painting – thereafter, provincial art is gradually absorbed into the grasp of the Moscow Kremlin workshop, its individuality expunged.

From middle Russia one can go south, of course, as well as north – though this may lead one into country all-too-easily

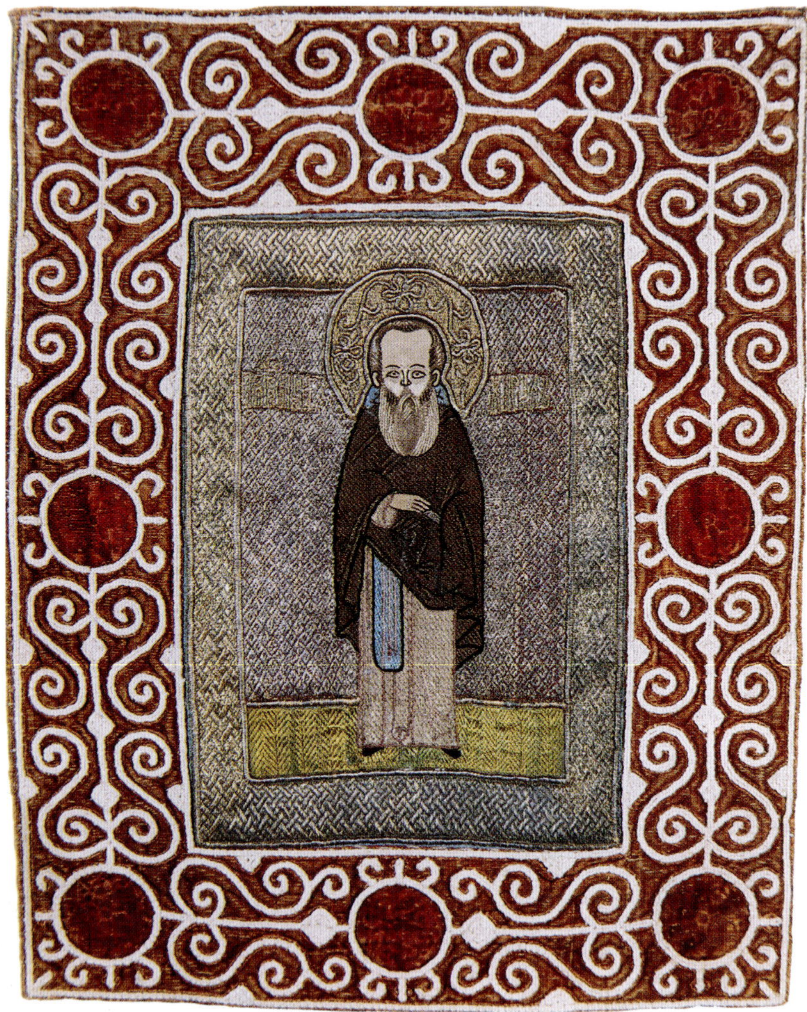

16 Dionisiy Glushitskiy, 1548, embroidered copy of a portrait-icon
representing St Kirill. The enterprising monk, painter, scribe and
wood-carver St Dionisiy Glushitskiy (1362–1437; coeval of Rublev),
founder of two monasteries on the Glushitsa river, painted a small
icon for the Kirillov Monastery depicting Kirill himself during his
lifetime (1424) – the first such direct portrait known in Russia. Its
popularity led to copies in various media: this embroidery in gold
thread was probably made for Ivan IV and his first wife, Anastasiya.

raided from the steppes. Around 150 kilometres south of Moscow the great river Oka flows west to east, marking a geographical border in earlier times. On the Oka, in the mid-fourteenth century, Moscow established two major strongpoints – the towns of Serpukhov and Kolomna – with their own monasteries and stone-built churches. We have no direct evidence that Rublev ever went there – yet, as a young man ready to learn the art of wall painting, maybe he did: in the 1380s there was no other work of the kind going on in Moscow itself.

Either way, he would have been very much aware of what took place in 1380. The Moscow Grand Prince Dmitriy Ivanovich led an all-Russian army southwards well beyond the Oka to the upper reaches of the Don, on the field of Kulikovo, to challenge a Tatar force led by Mamay. The politics of the occasion were fraught, and there was a sense that the Russians had overstepped limits, well captured by the major poet A. Blok (1880–1921) in his cycle 'On the Field of Kulikovo': 'I see a vast and silent conflagration raging far over Rus' ('Ya vizhu nad Rus'yu daleche/ Shirokiy i tikhiy pozhar'). But Dmitriy's army decisively won the day. Even though the situation with regard to paying tribute scarcely changed for a century, and there were several very destructive Tatar raids to come, Dmitriy had become a hero, now surnamed 'Donskoy'. Legend has it that Dmitriy had gone to the Trinity Monastery to seek Sergius's blessing for his expedition, and even that two Trinity monks had joined his forces (strictly against canon law). Actually this was not the first time a Russian army had defeated a Tatar one – only two years before this had happened at the river Vozha, close to modern Ryazan, eliciting swift revenge. But Kulikovo was the great set-piece following it up. It was commemorated in folklore and in a remarkable literary work discovered in various incomplete manuscripts in the nineteenth century and known as 'Zadonshchina' ('That which Happened Beyond the Don').

It turns out that the work was modelled on the 'Tale of the Armament of Igor', or 'Igor Tale', of two hundred years before – the highly poeticized account of the unsuccessful steppeland raid organized by the minor prince Igor Svyatoslavich (1185), on which Borodin's famous opera is based. It often uses similar phrases, but turns the story of an ignominious defeat at the hands of steppe people into one of victory, and a tale that used almost no Christian references into that of a Christian triumph against the infidel, a redressing of the historical balance; Polovtsians of the steppe are taken as equivalent to Tatars. Roman Jakobson has convincingly suggested that the two works constituted a diptych, to be read in conjunction with each other.[6] Here we can add that the written word – arriving at the Conversion – never lost a quality of sacredness in early Rus; its notable quantity of oral literature had to wait much longer before seeing print.

The cult of Dmitriy was well established by the time he died in 1389: he was informally called Tsar (that is, 'Caesar', the term used by Slavs for the emperor in Constantinople), his elder son Vasiliy was assured of the Grand Princely throne, he was in control of most of the central Russian principalities. It is clear from his will that he envisaged the possibility of no longer paying tribute to the Tatars. A remarkable and poetic encomium to him was composed after his death, partly inspired by the best writer of the day, Yepifaniy the Wise. He also fortified his city with stone walls: fortunately limestone quarries had recently been opened up at Myachkovo, downstream on the Moscow river.

All this cost money: tribute still needed to be paid to the Tatars, yet as a modern historian puts it, Moscow 'benefited from a general economic recovery that was evident in the Russian lands by the second half of the fourteenth century. Its vigorous construction programmes reflect an economic dynamism'[7] – this despite tribute payments, Tatar raids and successive waves of the Black Death. It is not easy to account for this. Moscow was (often) appointed chief tax-gatherer for the Tatars, and no doubt a poor tax-man is as rare as a hungry baker; it was also able, with northward expansion, to cream off some of Novgorod's wealth. The slash-and-burn agriculture required in such newly inhabited lands is actually rather productive, with its abundance of ash, for a few years at least; then farmers would move on. Perhaps, too, there was some climatic warming, though there is no firm evidence on this point.

From the fourteenth century, the Tatars were encouraging long-distance trade. One may conjecture that such trade could

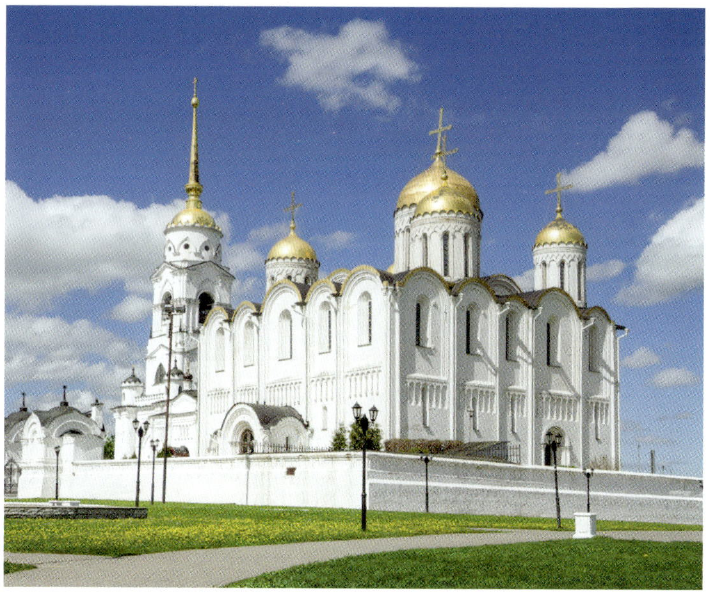

17 The 'Great Stone Church of the Mother of God in Vladimir', mother church of central Russia, looms above the river Klyazma, rising to the same height as Santa Sophia in Kiev (29 metres), one of several Kievan reminiscences in the city. Built under Andrey Bogolyubskiy in 1158–60, it was damaged by fire in 1185, but restored and enlarged on all sides in 1187, leading to a rather complicated interior. The Tatar attack of 1238 led to a further conflagration, leaving the cathedral in severe need of refurbishment; hence Daniil and Rublev's commission in 1408.

have brought Rublev's patrons the expensive lapis lazuli he used – in Western Europe it began to be supplied in the same period through Venice. Even in the Byzantine capital Moscow was considered worth touching for money: one of its highest church dignitaries, the Metropolitan of Trebizond, recorded as attending Dmitriy's funeral, was actually soliciting alms, as was another in 1407.[8] However it came about, the building of stone churches and palaces followed, and with it great opportunities for Rublev and colleagues.

Thus there was also a significant international dimension, irrespective of the Tatars, to Rublev's world: it stretched over the whole territory of the 'Byzantine Commonwealth'. The Great City itself, Constantinople, was the object of immense curiosity, but despite its Patriarch's ultimate authority over the Eastern Church, it no longer counted for so much politically. The Patriarch Antonios sent a tetchy letter to Grand Prince Vasiliy in the 1390s, complaining that the Eastern (that is, Byzantine) emperor's name was being left out of prayers: 'You cannot say "we have a church but not an emperor"' – but this was indeed possible, particularly when, at various points in the fourteenth and fifteenth centuries, the greatly diminished, often desperate empire tried to make deals with the Catholic West.

Meanwhile Russians could, and often did, travel to one or another monastery on the Holy Mountain of Athos in Northern Greece. But the most productive movement, as far as Russian cultural history was concerned, was northbound from the Balkan Slav kingdoms of Serbia and Bulgaria, already squeezed by the Ottoman Turks. Balkan churchmen (notably the Metropolitan Kiprian, instigator of the Trinity Chronicle, and his nephew Grigoriy Tsamblak, Metropolitan of Kiev) fitted easily into the Russian milieu, Pakhomy the Serb became Russia's first professional writer and at least two fourteenth-century churches in Novgorod were painted by Serbs or Bulgarians, while major changes in orthography, aiming to purify the Church Slavonic language, took place under South Slav influence.

There was a palpable sense of cultural renewal – indeed, Grigory Tsamblak triumphantly quotes 2 Corinthians 5: 'Behold, all things are made new,' in connection with his own translations and other writings. D. S. Likhachov was the first to describe this as a near-universal manifestation within the 'Byzantine-Slav cultural milieu' in his brilliant essay on 'The Culture of Russia in the Age of Andrey Rublev and Yepifaniy the Wise'.[9] In it, besides these two main figures, he touches on architecture, church life, music and much else, finding in each cultural realm a sense of renewal and heightened individualism; beyond that, an urge to restore lost glories of the pre-Tatar past.

An aspect of this urge must have been the refurbishment of the Dormition Cathedral in Vladimir, to which Rublev and Daniil made such a notable contribution (illus. 17, 39–51). A little later, in the mid-fifteenth century, the Grand Prince Ivan III instigated the very difficult restoration of the thirteenth-century ruined St George at Yuriev-Polskiy (originally 'Polskoy'), its exterior covered in carvings, while in Novgorod Archbishop Euthemius II undertook an even more extensive restoration programme. The binding medium in all this activity of renovation, in the Balkans as in Russia, was the Church Slavonic language – no longer spoken, as it had been in the days of Cyril and Methodius, Apostles to the Slavs (ninth century), but nowhere incomprehensible, and never regarded as 'other', as Latin was in medieval England. Eventually it would be a major component of the Russian literary language as formulated in the early eighteenth century.

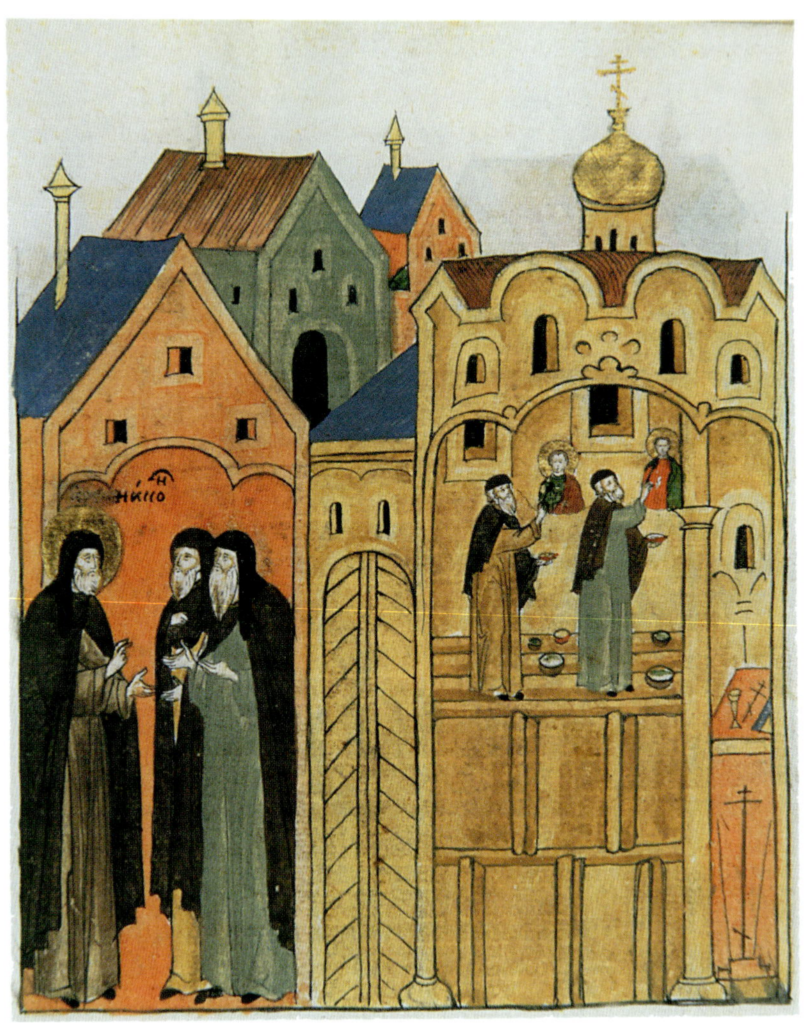

18 Andrey and Daniil at work (on a wooden platform) painting the Dormition Cathedral in Vladimir, from an illustrated chronicle compendium (1570s/80s).

FOUR

Life and Works

All commentators place Rublev's birth between 1360 and 1370. A date before the former might be conceivable, but for various reasons is improbable; after the latter, and the comment that he died 'at a great age' – though working to near the end – would be unlikely. In the USSR his six-hundredth anniversary was celebrated in 1960, and led to exhibitions and many publications. Where he came from is unknown. His surname, not very usual at the time, could have been derived from a place (there is still a settlement called Rublyovo to the west of Moscow, and another near Yaroslavl), but more probably relates to a family trade: a *rubel* was a tool used in processing animal hides.[10]

At some point he became a monk, probably at the Trinity Monastery or its offshoot close to Moscow, the Andronikov, even though at the time most painters were laymen; it is possible he was shorn in middle age. In any case, as mentioned above, the only contemporary chronicle records of him refer to 1405 and 1408 – participating in what must have been highly important commissions for Vasiliy 1 – by which time he must have been an accomplished painter. The brief records read, first, 'The same spring the stone church of the Annunciation at the Grand Prince's court began to be painted – not the one now standing – and the masters were Feofan (Theophanes) the Greek, Prokhor the elder from Gorodets, and the monk Andrey Rublev,

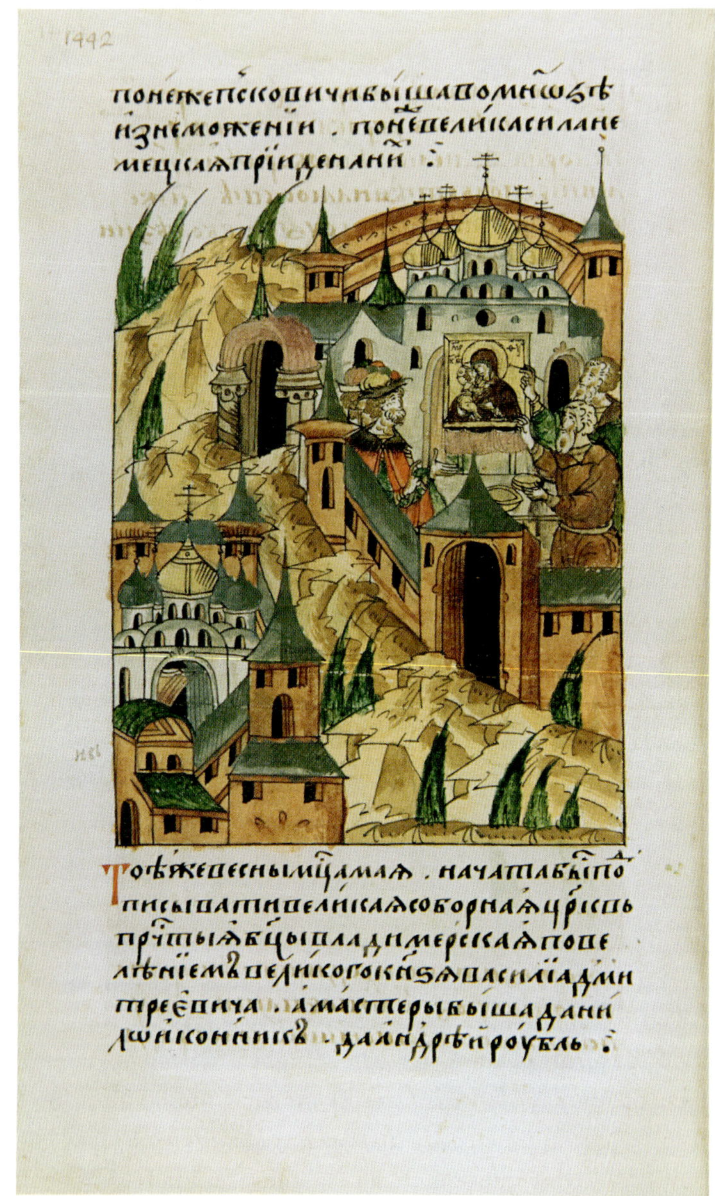

19 Andrey and Daniil at work on the Dormition Cathedral, Vladimir, from an illustrated chronicle compendium (1570s/80s).

and it was finished the same year'; second, 'The same year on 25 May the great stone cathedral church of the Mother of God in Vladimir began to be painted, at the command of the Grand Prince, and the masters were Danilo the icon painter and Andrey Rublev.'

Rublev's is the final name in each case, doubtless indicating that he was the youngest; it is worth noting that there would have been apprentices and assistants, making up a *druzhina* or team, at work too. The Vladimir commission, of course, was a restoration job, and one of high prestige (illus. 19; see illus. 17). The great cathedral, 'Mother Church' of middle Russia, had been seriously damaged by fire, though a few twelfth-century paintings survived. Rublev and Daniil basically repainted the central part and supervised the construction of the immense icon screen: an inventory of 1708 lists 83 icons (of which only nineteen now remain with the original paintwork). One of the foremost specialists has written that it 'was the greatest of all iconostases made in medieval Russia . . . apparently it was Rublev and his assistants who first created a grandiose multi-tier iconostasis' – an invention that permanently changed the Orthodox church interior.[11] This one was dismantled in 1774, and its icons were sold off to the people of a local village; we are lucky that any survive. The frescoes that have lasted to our day form the larger part of a complex Last Judgement, often hard to make out by eye – modern candle smoke has not helped.

Who painted what? There seem to be two hands at work in the wall paintings: the larger part of them by a younger painter, a few by an older. Maybe Daniil Chorniy (that is, 'Black'), if described as an *ikonnik* or icon painter, largely stuck with the icons. Who can say? Anyhow, he and Andrey struck up a friendship that lasted the rest of their lives, so their respective artistic manners must have been in accord with each other. It is worth noting that although there were plenty of icons in the form of panel paintings in Russia at the time, wall paintings (inappropriate in wooden buildings) were rare, except in Novgorod's stone churches.

Several times immigrant painters were hired for such painterly tasks. Feofan the Greek was such a one, and a man of clearly unusual gifts and vigour, about whom more will be said. Doubtless already in his seventies, he disappears from the historical record after the work at the Annunciation Cathedral. About Prokhor we know nothing more – not even which of several places called Gorodets he came from; it has been speculated that he was Rublev's teacher. It was long thought that, although the Annunciation Cathedral was rebuilt in 1416 and then completely burnt down in the mid-sixteenth century, its former iconostasis must have been saved from the flames (despite this being contradicted in the chronicle sources). But during a major restoration programme in the 1980s, the icon screen was thoroughly examined, and a stranger truth emerged: part of the screen (icons representing the Feast Days) is now attributed to the early fifteenth century, part (the Deisis range) to the late fourteenth, other icons to the sixteenth.[12] Innumerable tour guides, confidently dividing the existing icons between Feofan, Rublev and Prokhor, have had to relearn their scripts. The rest of us can breathe a sigh of relief – these were not top-quality works. Of course, it cannot be excluded that Rublev and/or Feofan made some of them, though it seems unlikely. It can be assumed that, in restoring the screen, Ivan iv brought in old icons from a source unknown to us today – possibly the Nativity Cathedral, no longer extant, but painted by Feofan and one Simeon Chorniy in 1395 (did 'Simeon the Black' perhaps become 'Daniil the Black' on being shorn a monk?).

Our information on Rublev becomes less certain beyond the curiously precise information about the Grand Princely commissions of 1405 and 1408, depending as it does on the lives of

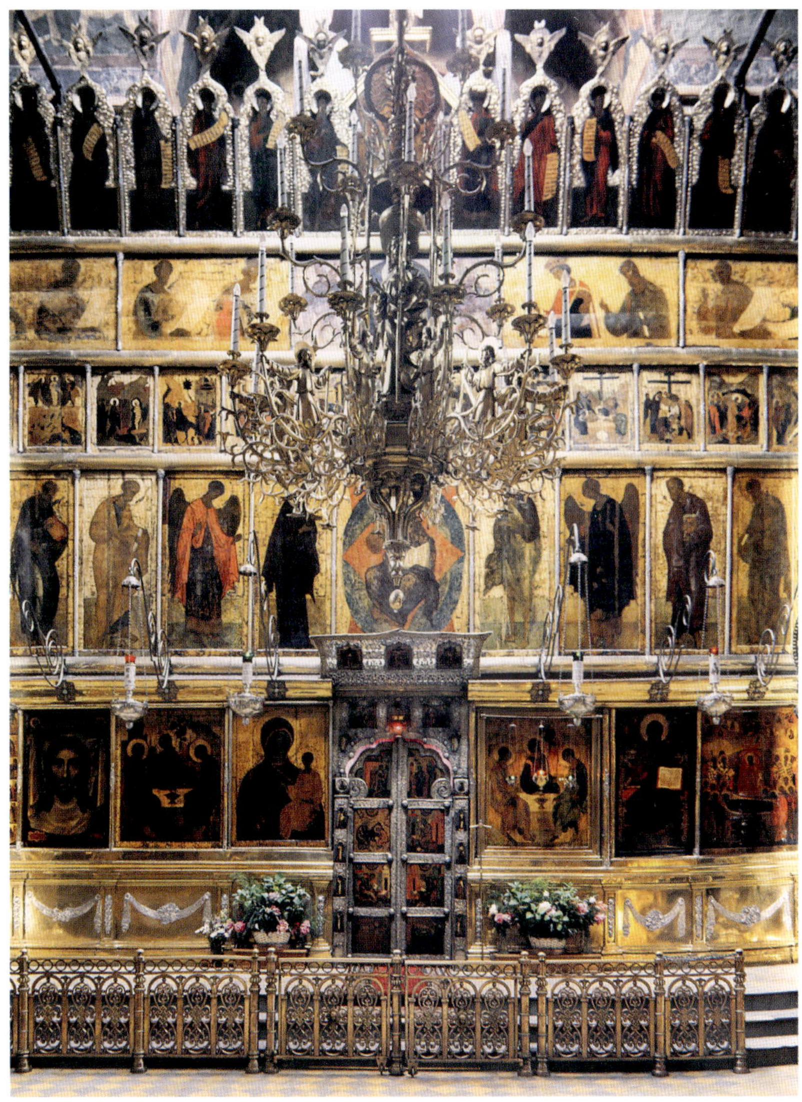

20 Workshop of Daniil and Rublev, iconostasis of the Trinity Monastery cathedral, 1422/3. The oldest 'high' icon screen still in situ. Lowest tier: 'local' icons (once containing the *Old Testament Trinity*; now a reproduction); above that, the Deisus tier; above that, 'Feast Day' tier; above that, Prophets; top, Patriarchs – these figures, in ornate casings, from *c.* 1600.

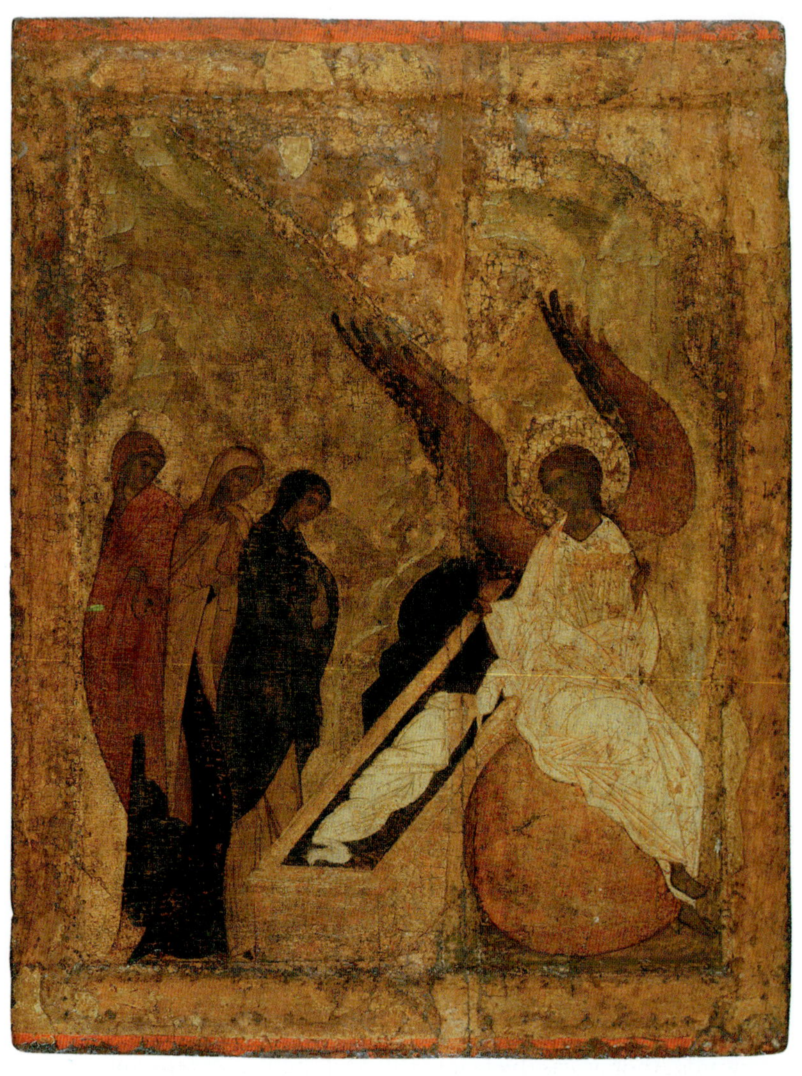

21 'Women at the Tomb', from the 'Feast Day' tier of Trinity Monastery, *c.* 1425; this vivid scene is no doubt from the hand of a younger assistant in the team.

Sergius and his successor Nikon. In 1425 the Trinity Monastery at last acquired a stone-built church, which stands to this day. Nikon, sensing his end was approaching, got Rublev and Daniil to paint it, in something of a hurry (illus. 18). Their wall paintings were, sadly, replaced in the seventeenth century, but the iconostasis – the oldest surviving complete 'high' one – is still intact (illus. 20). For almost five hundred years the great *Old Testament Trinity* painted in memory of Sergius (according to a seventeenth-century source) stood there, immediately to the right of the royal doors; otherwise the icons, some now in poor condition, seem to have been largely painted, or finished, by assistants (illus. 21).

Finally, in the last years of the 1420s, Rublev returned to the relatively small Andronikov Monastery near Moscow. The abbot, Alexander, conferred with the brethren and – according to the life of Nikon – together with Rublev planned a 'very beautiful' church, which 'they painted with their own hands, and stands to this day'. It is not only (after judicious restoration: the upper part had collapsed in 1812) the oldest building in Moscow, but the finest and most elaborate in the early Muscovite style that survives (illus. 22). Its interior lost its plaster and much of its roof, but a pair of narrow windows, formerly blocked, were opened up at restoration in 1959/61 and found to retain painted ornaments on the splays – Rublev's final legacy? (illus. 23). No mention here of Daniil, but all later sources recount, rather sentimentally if touchingly, how soon afterwards Andrey was the first to die, and then appeared, shining brilliantly, to summon his colleague to join him 'in great joy' (illus. 24).

There are other commissions that Rublev is believed most likely to have had. The greatest of these, without doubt, is the Zvenigorod range. The story is well known: an expedition in 1918 to explore the artistic legacy of this little town west of

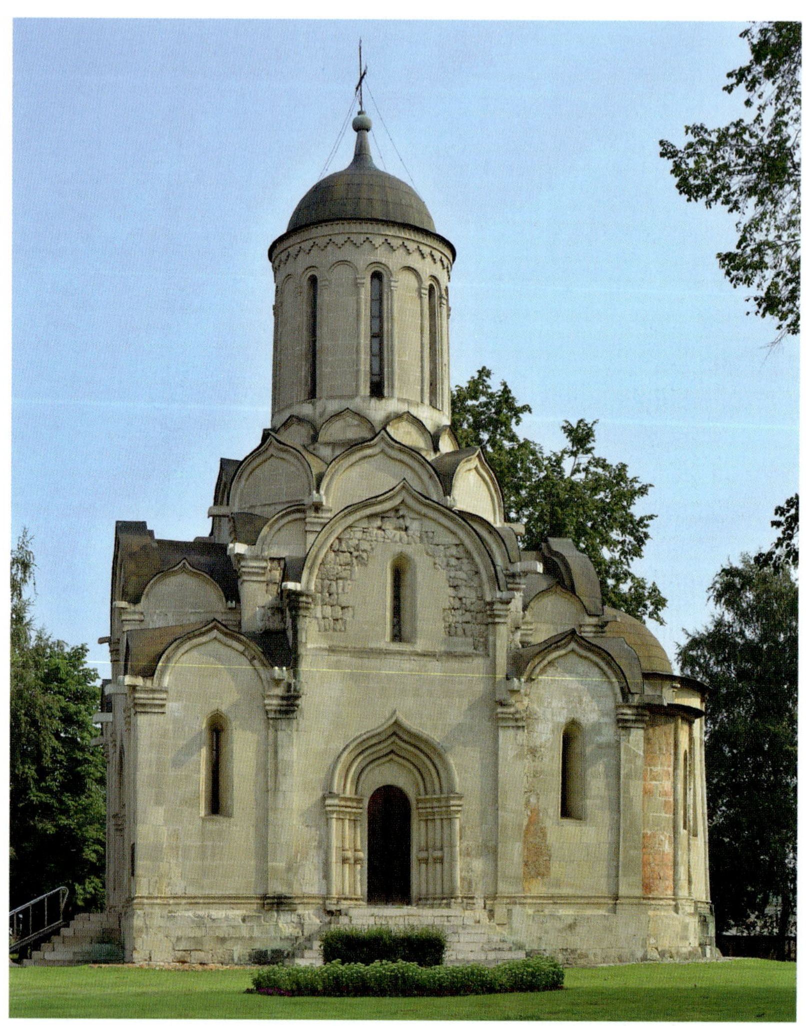

22 Andronikov Monastery of the Saviour, *c.* 1427, the most complex
and elegant early Muscovite building, and today the oldest free-standing
structure in Moscow, located above the small Yauza river on the main road
east. The abbot Alexander consulted with the brethren on its building;
Rublev, by then a senior and highly respected figure, undertook its painting
(of which only a pair of window splays remain). The church was severely
damaged in the French occupation of 1812 and partially burnt; the upper
parts collapsed but were satisfactorily restored in 1959–60 (differences in
stonework make this apparent). Since 1947 the monastery has been the
Andrey Rublev Museum of Old Russian Art.

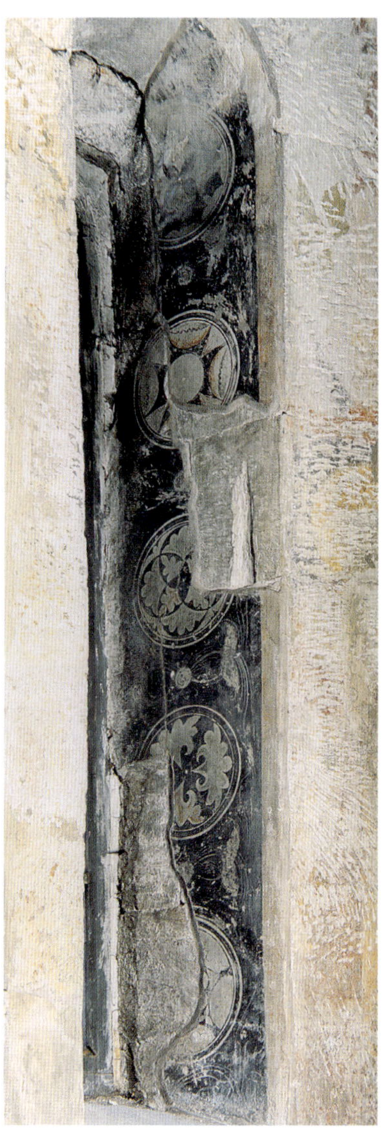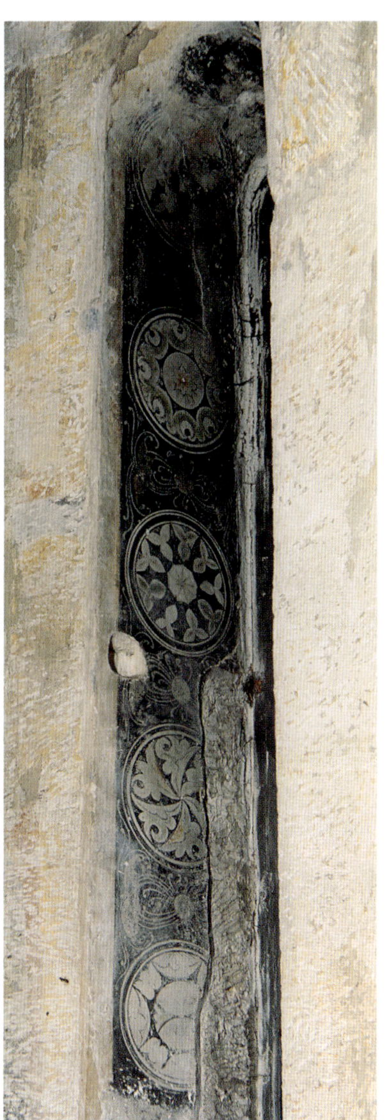

23 Andronikov Monastery, Moscow: two window splays, painted by Rublev, late 1420s. From Rublev's final commission, there remain only the splays of two narrow windows at the east end, with their elegant decoration of varied medallions. They were bricked up in the 16th century, survived the fire of 1812, and were revealed only in 1952 (since when their colour is reported to have considerably faded).

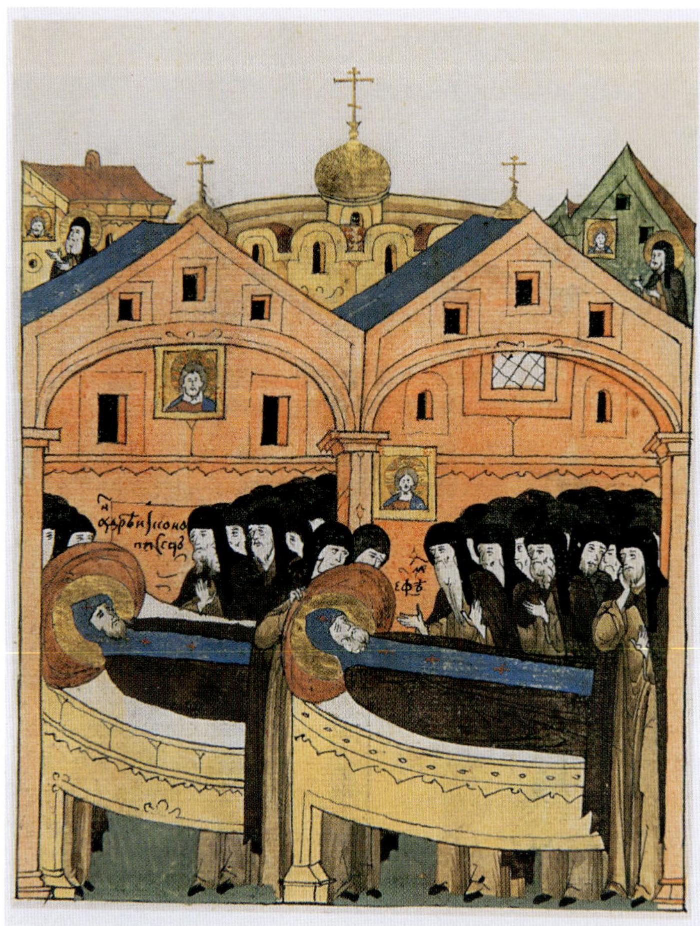

24 Imagined scene of the deaths of Abbot Alexander and Andrey Rublev at the Andronikov Monastery, from an illuminated edition of *Life of St Sergius* (1580s–early 1590s). Alexander died in 1427 or 1428, so casting doubt on Rublev's gravestone giving his death as 1430. Another account has Rublev and his companion Daniil dying at almost the same time.

Moscow came upon three magnificent, if much damaged, icons in a woodshed near the small but ancient Dormition Cathedral (*c.* 1399). Why there? Because Dmitriy Donskoy in his will left Zvenigorod as an appanage principality to his second son, Yuriy, who (also owning the larger, remoter territory of Galich) prospered and set up his own court. Yuriy had close connections with the Trinity Monastery (illus. 26, 27, 29).

The quality of the painting – and similarities with the *Old Testament Trinity* – have never put the attribution to Rublev in serious doubt, yet questions have arisen. How could these large icons have fitted into an icon-range in either this cathedral, or that of the Savvino-Storozhevsky Monastery nearby, with its church of circa 1404? They show half-length figures, so cannot be part of a high iconostasis, but would fit onto a

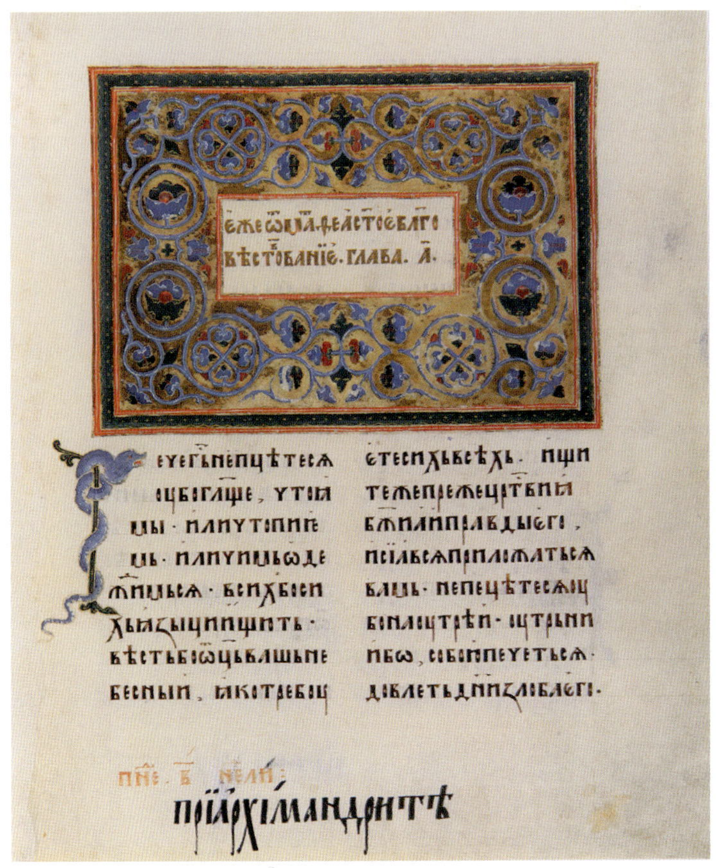

25 Heading of St Matthew's Gospel, with serpentine initial, from the Khitrovo gospel book, early 15th century.

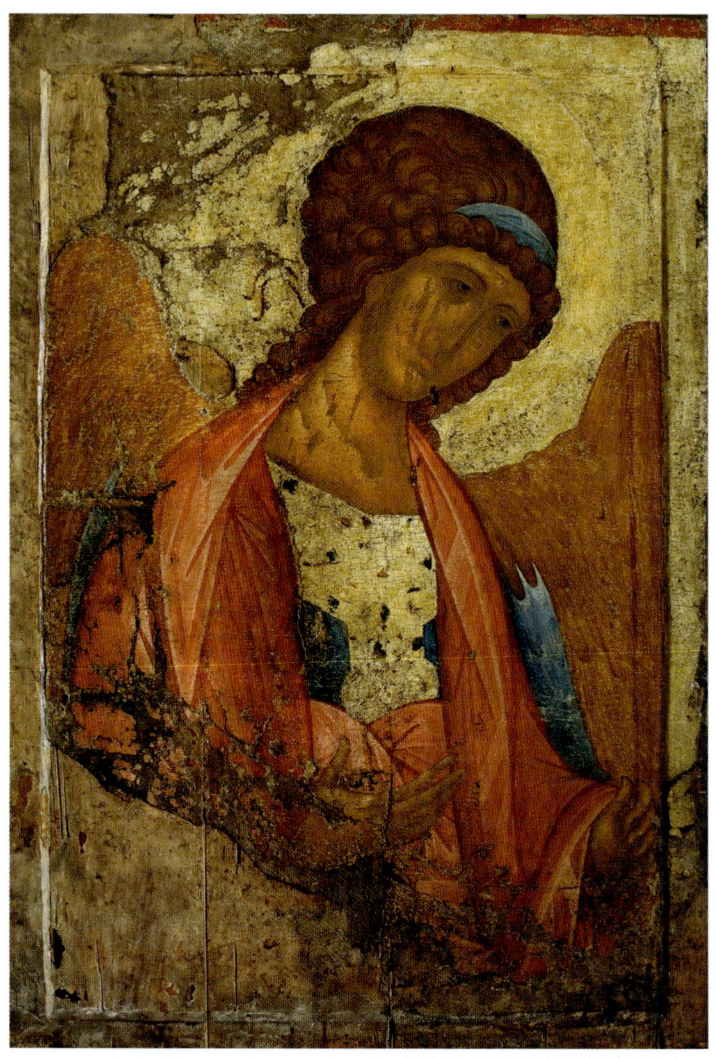

26 Zvenigorod range (attrib. to Rublev), *St Michael*, c. 1400. The range
of half-length icons in the Cathedral of the Dormition on the Hill
once numbered seven (possibly nine), of which three carrying original
paintwork survive – found, we are told, in a nearby woodshed by an
expedition under the direction of Igor Grabar in October 1918. The
most dazzling of these – with brilliant splashes of red and blue – is that of
St Michael. It is calm and tender, its angelic rather than military features
accentuated (unlike, for example, the one of similar date by Feofan's

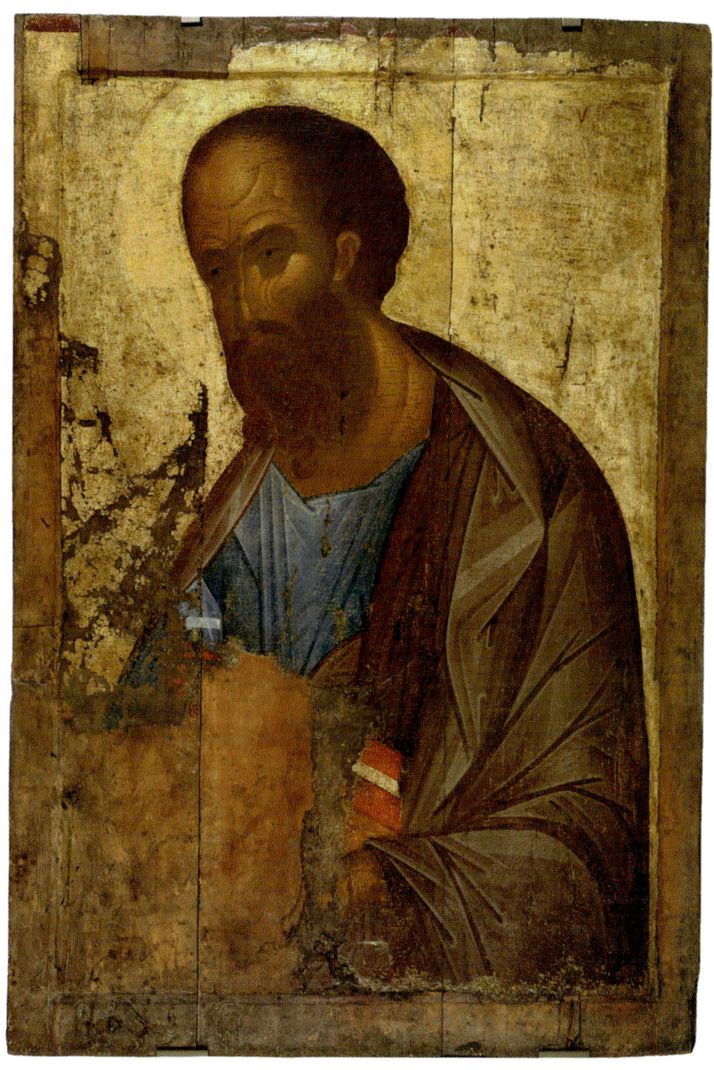

team). The head is so close to those of the angels in the *Old Testament Trinity*, and figures in the Vladimir paintings, that few have doubted the attribution to Rublev. The patron, Prince Yuriy of Zvenigorod, had close ties with the Trinity-Sergius Monastery. Part of the woven cloth underlay is exposed beneath the figure.

27 Zvenigorod range (attrib. to Rublev), *St Paul, c.* 1400. The colder tones of the dignified and statuesque St Paul have led some specialists to attribute this icon to Daniil or to a follower.

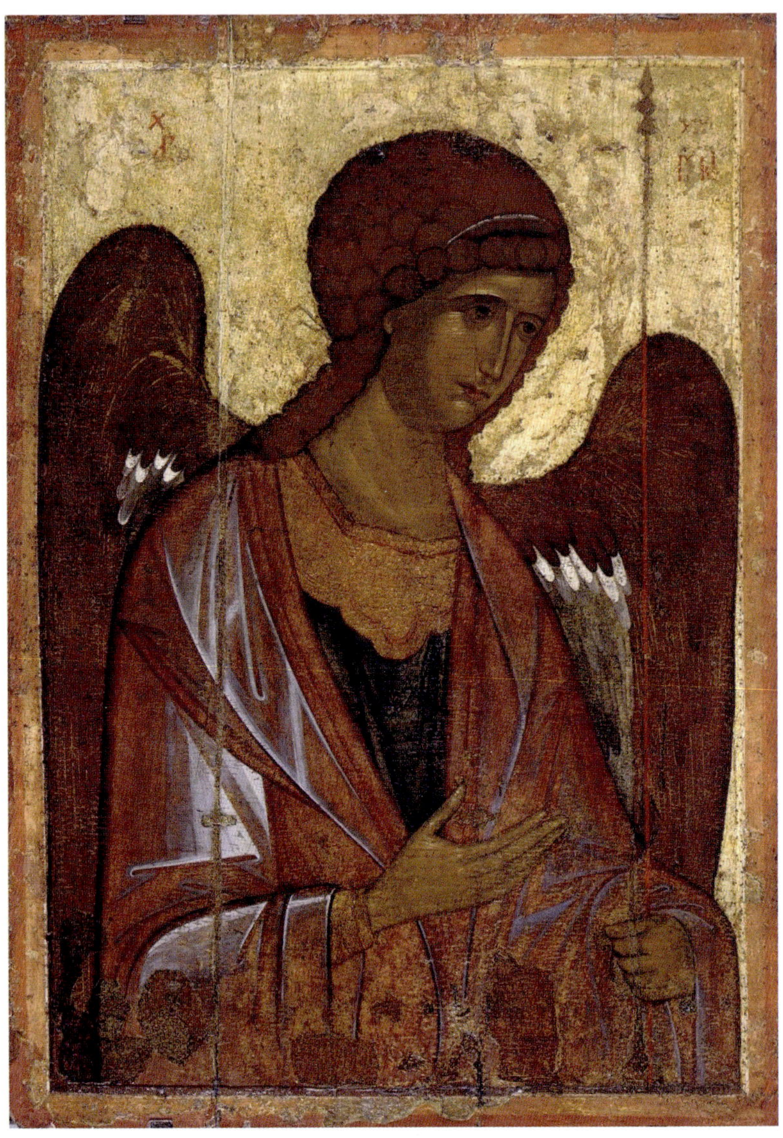

28 Vysotskiy range, *St Michael*, late 14th century, from a set of
half-length icons imported from Byzantium for the Vysotskiy
Monastery, Kolomna, which partially survives, and may have
served as an inspiration for the Zvenigorod range; the tilt of
the head and gestures are not unlike those of St Michael there,
though the Zvenigorod icon is far subtler and more 'finished'.

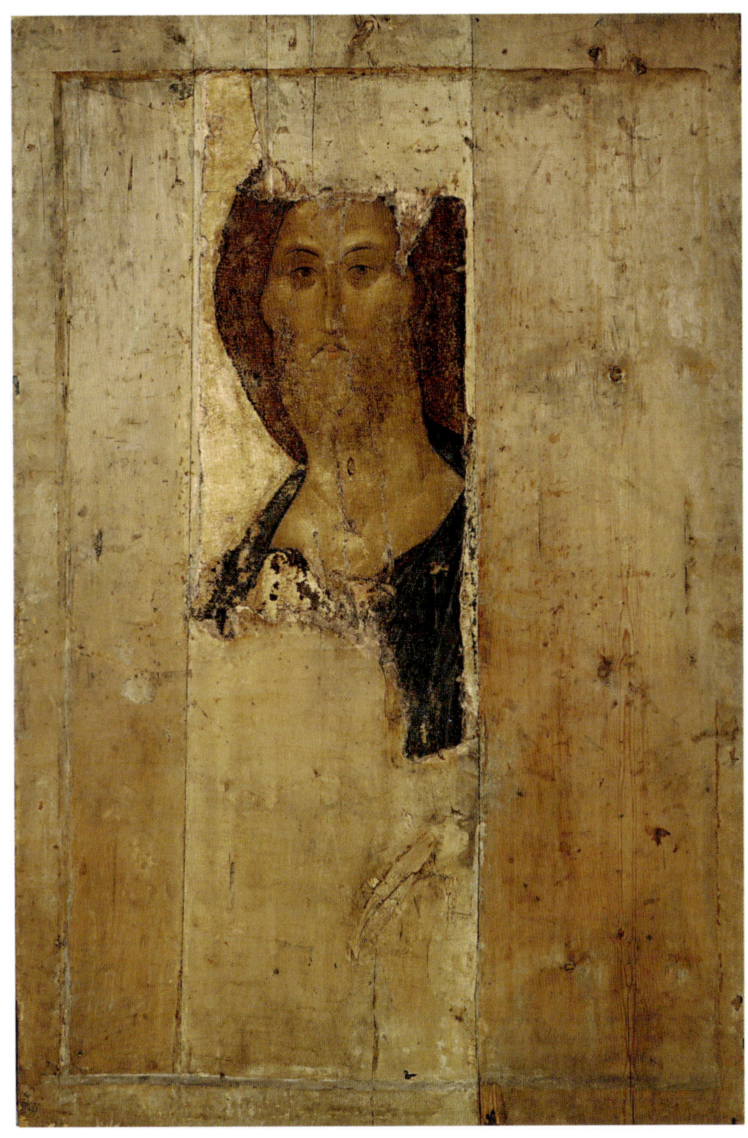

29 Zvenigorod range (attrib. to Rublev), *The Saviour*, *c.* 1400.
This central icon has lost more paint than the other two; the
right-hand board (pine, not lime) is a 20th-century replacement.
Enough survives, however, to appreciate its grave yet unthreatening
presence.

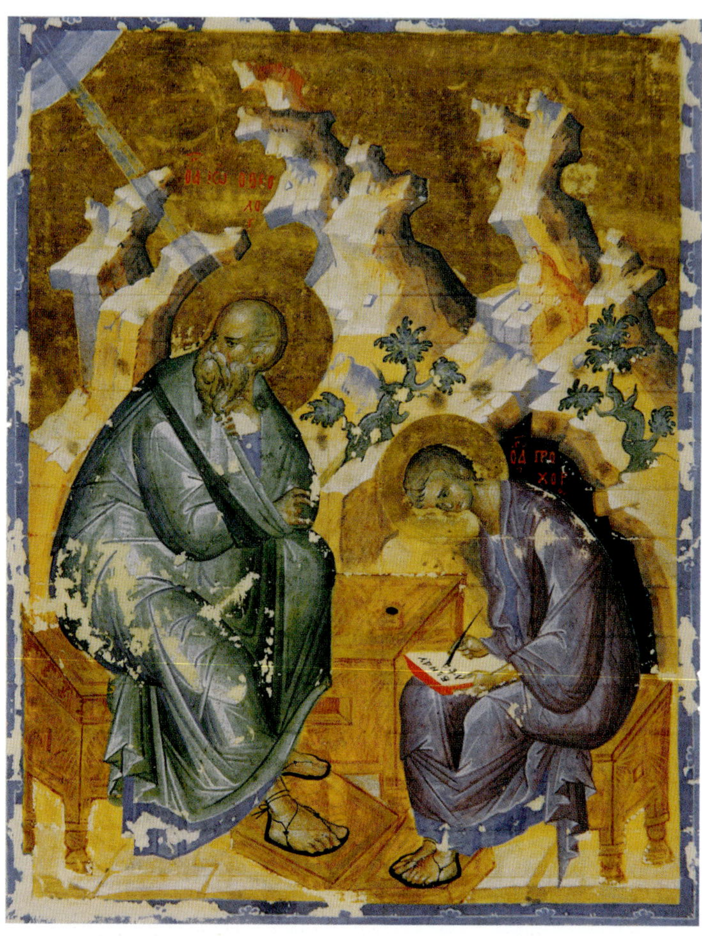

30 St John, illustration from the Khitrovo gospel book, early 15th century. The Evangelist and his scribe Prochoros receive inspiration on the mountainous island of Patmos, amid a marvellously contorted rocky landscape.

templon (this is the term used in Byzantine art history for a low screen demarcating the sanctuary, on which icons were often placed). An inventory made in the 1690s tells us that the range then contained seven icons, and that they were, unusually, set round the walls of the church. These half-length figures could be in imitation or emulation of the Vysotsky range, imported

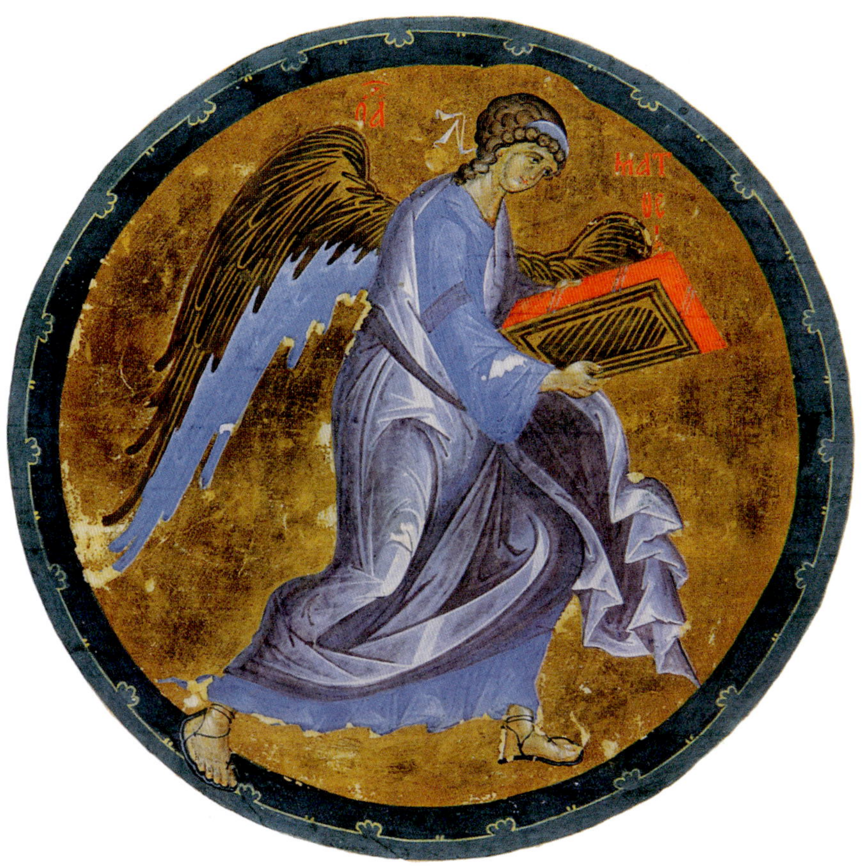

31 St Matthew, illustration from the Khitrovo gospel book, one of half
a dozen splendid gospel manuscripts on parchment that survive from the
opening years of the 15th century; it is suggested they were produced
for use in the main Moscow churches. Their general decoration derives
from Byzantine examples, but they are of unusually fine quality, in
immaculate, semi-uncial, sometimes decorated script. By general
consent the finest is the Khitrovo book (so named after a 17th-century
boyar who donated it to the Trinity Monastery). As well as rectangular
illustrations of the Evangelists at work, there are beguiling roundels
containing their symbols, and headings with neo-Byzantine decorative
motifs. The leading Moscow artists must have been drawn into this
operation. The roundel of St Matthew's symbol (an angel) is particularly
close to Rublev's manner, its gravity offset by the discreet interruption
of the circumference at head and foot.

from Constantinople to the Serpukhov Vysotsky Monastery around 1390 (illus. 28) – and greatly superior to them. The figures are so accomplished that it is difficult to imagine them as relatively early works, circa 1400, yet such they seem to be.

From a similar or perhaps slightly later date comes the stunning Khitrovo gospel book (so named after the boyar Khitrovo, who in the 1670s presented it to the Trinity Monastery). At some point at the start of the fifteenth century half a dozen magnificently ornamented parchment gospel books – deriving from, and if anything outdoing, earlier Byzantine and South Slav examples

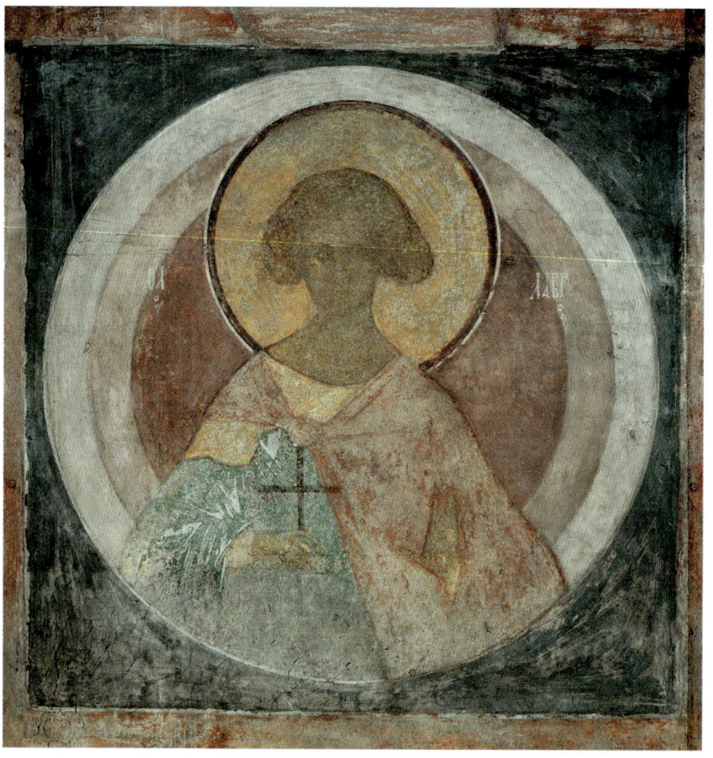

32 St Lavr (=Lauros; with Floros, martyr-saints, taken by Russians as protectors of horses), fragmentary wall painting in Zvenigorod Dormition Cathedral, c. 1399, often attributed to Rublev, and if so an early work by him.

– were produced, probably to be placed in the main Moscow cathedrals (illus. 25, 30, 31). For their fine miniatures and initials the best talents available in Moscow must have been brought in, by then including Rublev. The almost identical Morozov gospel book is evidently an imitation, slightly less masterful in all respects. Commentators have had a field day trying to establish what role, if any, Rublev played in the illumination of the Khitrovo gospel book: one may as well go along with M. V. Alpatov's opinion that 'if Rublev did not paint most of its scenes, one has to posit another artist working in Moscow at the time, as like him as his own brother.'[13] Vzdornov associates two more of these gospel books with Rublev's immediate circle.[14] It should be added that many other works over the years have been attributed to Rublev – including some remains of wall paintings in the two early Zvenigorod churches (illus. 32) – but none match the Zvenigorod icon-range or Khitrovo book in significance. The latter, incidentally, if its illustrations are accepted as by Rublev, is the only work in his canon that can reasonably be described as largely in good condition.

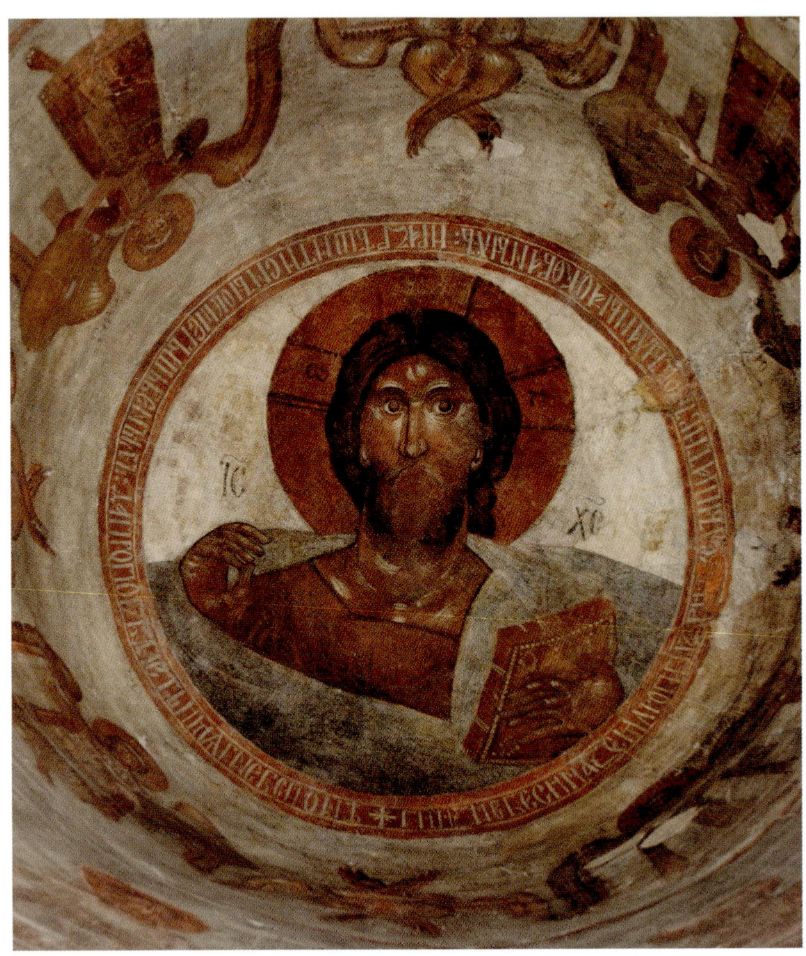

33 Feofan Grek, *Pantocrator* ('Ruler of All'), 1378. The face of Christ Pantocrator rather alarmingly dominates the interior space of the Novgorod merchants' Church of the Transfiguration of the Saviour on Ilyin Street from its place in the centre of the dome.

FIVE

Rublev as Artist

In the past I have inveighed against too-ready use of the terms 'art' and 'artist' in respect of medieval figures, for whom these general concepts did not exist – or at any rate lacked specific words in Old Russian.[15] Perhaps, though, the time of Rublev marks the stage at which 'art', with its concomitants of unified artistic vision and personality, begins to form – as indeed with Italian *trecento* painters such as Duccio and Simone Martini. Rublev is so distinctive, whether as fresco painter, icon painter, book illuminator or even designer of a building, that one should look at the totality of his artistic achievement. He never exceeded the bounds of his own East Christian conceptual world, yet showed how new things can be achieved within it. Nevertheless, the paucity of information about Rublev may lead one to assume that there are few or no avenues by which we can form any idea of how a painter of his period saw himself or his modus operandi, or indeed how either were seen by others.

Such an assumption, however, would be mistaken. A remarkable document from Rublev's lifetime survives, one that brings the reader more closely into the world of art than one might have any hope of expecting – in the form of a letter from 'one Yepifaniy' to a friend of his, Kirill. The former is generally accepted as being Yepifaniy the Wise, the recipient, Kirill, abbot of a monastery in Tver. It makes no mention of Rublev, yet relates rather closely to him, in that both the sender and the subject of it were people he had known well. To get the full feel of it, a complete translation is required. Its manuscript, by the way, was found in the archive of Anzer skete on the Solovki archipelago, and has never been put in doubt.

Copied from a letter sent by the Hieromonk Yepifaniy to a friend of his, Kirill.

You have seen the Constantinople church of Sophia illustrated in my Gospel book, in Greek called Tetraevangelion, in our Russian language the Four Gospels. This is how it came about that the building was drawn in our book. When I was living in Moscow, there lived there a splendidly wise man, a very clever philosopher, Feofan, by birth a Greek, a skilled book illustrator, and as an icon-painter a wonderful artist, who painted more than forty stone-built churches with his own hand, in the cities of Constantinople, Chalcedon, Galata, Kaffa, in Novgorod the Great and Nizhniy Novgorod. In Moscow, too, three churches were painted by him: the Annunciation of the Holy Mother of God, St Michael and one more. In St Michael he depicted a city on the wall, portraying all its details with his paints; at Prince Vladimir Andreyevich's residence he depicted Moscow itself on a stone wall; the palace of the Grand Prince was painted with an extraordinary and wonderful scene; and in the stone church of the Annunciation he also painted a 'Tree of Jesse' and an 'Apocalypse'.

When he depicted or drew all this, nobody saw him ever looking at models, as do some of our icon painters, who without comprehension stare at them continually, looking hither and thither, and do not so much paint with colours as gaze at the models. He however makes

the painting with his hands, as it were, while continually
moving around, talking with visitors and pondering
something lofty and wise in his mind, and with the insight
of his reason witnesses the goodness reason brings. This
marvellous and outstanding man conceived a great
affection for my unworthiness; and I, unworthy and foolish
as I was, found the courage often to visit him to converse,
since conversing with him was something I loved.

Whoever made conversation with him, whether briefly
or at length, could not but be struck by his wisdom, his
clever way of speaking and his intelligent frame of mind.
When I saw that he liked me and didn't despise me, I added
shamelessness to my boldness, and asked him: 'I beg your
wisdom to paint me the great Sophia in Constantinople,
the one the great emperor Justinian built, vying with
Solomon the wise king; some say that in size and quality
it is like the Moscow Kremlin within our city, so large is it
when you walk around it: if a visitor comes in and wants to
explore without a guide, he'll never get out without losing
himself, intelligent as he might seem to be – in view of the
multitude of columns and their surroundings, entrances
and passageways, various rooms and chapels, stairways
and storerooms, tombs, variously-named subdivisions and
additions, ways in and out, and stone pillars too. Paint me
the aforesaid Justinian seated on his horse, and holding in
his right hand a copper apple whose size is such that you
can pour two and a half buckets of water into it, so they
say – and show all this on one sheet, so that I can put it
at the beginning of my book, and remembering your work
and looking at the holy place I can imagine myself in
Constantinople.'

Being a wise man, he answered me wisely: 'It is impossible
either for you to have this, or for me to paint it – but at

your insistence I shall draw it for you partially: even that will be not so much a part, as a hundredth portion, a tiny bit of a great thing; but thanks to this tiny bit drawn by me you will be able to imagine and understand the rest.' Saying this, he boldly took up his brush and swiftly drew a picture of the holy place, just like the real church in Constantinople, and gave it to me. That sheet was very useful to other Moscow icon painters as well, since many copied it for themselves, competing among each other and vying with one another. Thereafter I too followed them as an artist, drew four views of it, and we placed it in our book at four places: [a] at the beginning of the book, in St Matthew's Gospel, where there is the column of Justinian, and a picture of St Matthew; [b] at the beginning of St Mark; [c] before the beginning of St Luke; [d] before the beginning of St John's Gospel – I drew four holy places and four evangelists, which you saw when I, alarmed by Edigey, escaped to Tver, found repose with you and told you of my misfortune, and showed you all the books left to me from my escape and confusion. Then it was that you saw the drawing of the holy place, and six years later, last winter, were kind enough to remind me of it.[16]

This remarkable personal letter – in tone quite unlike the few other surviving letters of the time, such as those of Metropolitan Kiprian, and datable from its last sentence to 1415 – may deserve closer analysis than would be appropriate here, but any reader can feel its mixture of wit and seriousness, the insight it gives into how monks and painters actually thought and talked.

It leaves one or two tantalizing questions unanswered: what can the 'extraordinary and wonderful' picture the Grand Prince was honoured with have been? Did Feofan learn anything new

in Galata or Kaffa, both Genoese colonies? (There is no subsequent sign he did.) But it also evokes a sobering thought: out
of the forty-odd churches Feofan evidently painted, with a few
palaces thrown in for good measure, only a single one survives,
and that fragmentarily – the Church of the Transfiguration of
the Saviour on Ilyin Street in Novgorod (1378). Without it
one would have little idea how one of the leading – and most
original – artists of the fourteenth century painted (we can be
all the more grateful that anything at all has survived from the
brush of Feofan's younger colleague, Rublev). How did Feofan
paint, then? And how does our response relate to Rublev?

The answer is disconcerting. From the Novgorod frescoes,
as well as a few icons that seem to have come at least from his
workshop, it is clear that Feofan was every bit as individual as
Yepifaniy's account would have us believe, and in a direction
that seems to run counter to all that we know about Rublev.
Like Gogol's tailor Petrovich in his story 'The Overcoat', he
'loved strong effects', and the Church of the Transfiguration has
them in abundance. Most figures are represented hieratically, in
solemn but never identical poses. Dark colours – particularly a
'brick earth' red – predominate, lit up by weird streaks and highlights of white, as if the whole were caught in a flash of lightning.

This is equally true of the three or four remarkable Moscow
icons that are attributed to his workshop (illus. 34, 35). I cannot
resist a personal anecdote: when I visited the church in 1990 it
was under restoration; a tottering wooden walkway led across
the building to the final ladder, reaching a wooden platform in
the drum of the dome, scarcely held up on the original masonry
high above the stone floor. Here I was suddenly face-to-face
with Feofan's terrifying Pantocrator (Christ as All-Ruler), sur-
rounded by huge figures of saints and prophets – much damaged
in the War, since the dome had held a German lookout post. I
didn't linger (illus. 33).

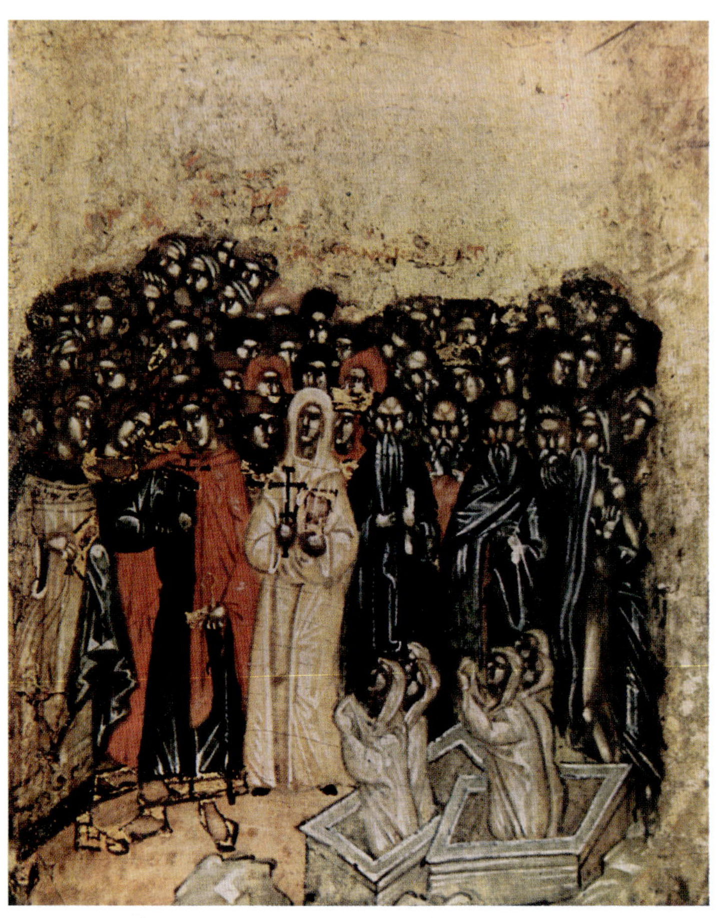

34 Feofan Grek (or follower), one scene from a small four-part icon, late 14th century, showing the dead arising in preparation for the Last Judgement in a highly dramatic, even expressionistic manner, with daring use of Feofan's characteristic white highlights. Found in the Moscow belfry 'Ivan the Great' in 1918.

35 Feofan Grek (or follower), *Dormition of the Mother of God* (backed by the Virgin of the Don), third quarter of 14th century, from Dormition Cathedral, Kolomna, a startlingly original version of a scene usually thronged with bystanders and the Heavenly Host. Here a candle represents the soul of the Mother of God, whose body is borne aloft as an infant by Christ.

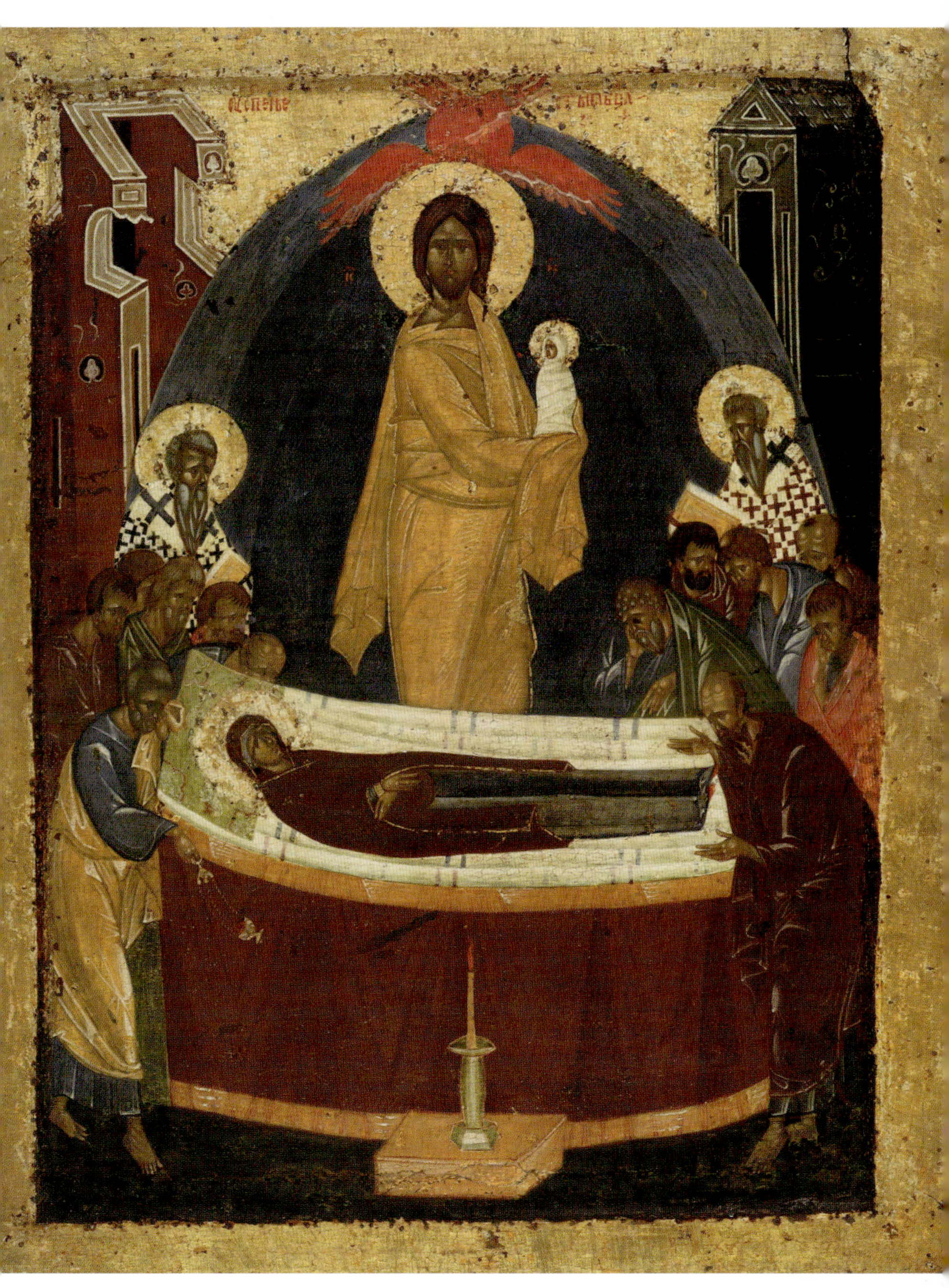

Успѣнье
Бцы

Feofan's presence in Novgorod in the late 1370s seems to have had a considerable effect on local painters: the Church of the Dormition on Volotovo Field (reduced to rubble in the war) and of St Theodore Stratilates (both 1380s) have, or had, equally strange, individualistic and dramatic pictorial schemes (illus. 36). How could Rublev, a junior member of Feofan's team working on the Moscow Annunciation Cathedral, not have been equally influenced? Of course over a quarter-century had elapsed since the Transfiguration church was painted, and maybe Feofan had softened in old age – though Yepifaniy's letter would suggest otherwise. Commentators are divided on this: some indeed make the two artists out to be antipodes – a curious thought, if they were perched side-by-side on scaffolding. Nonetheless Rublev's characteristic style is harmonious, with a predilection for rounded forms, thoughtful, undemonstrative facial types, balanced compositions. Stylistically he is as remote from Feofan's dynamic mode as you could imagine, even if a modern Byzantinist surprisingly claims that 'the work of Rublev and his followers depends directly on the work of Theophanes.'[17]

Yet Feofan could have taught him two or three things. First, the painterly ease and fluency that emerges from Yepifaniy's account. Second, thoughtfulness, 'inner contemplation', in all his work: an inner contemplation that is closely tied up with the Hesychast teaching of God's perceptible energies in the form of light, differently as Feofan and Rublev approach this. Third, the classical impulse that Feofan would have picked up from his Greek heritage, brought up as he must have been in the early Palaeologan age, with its strongly classicizing tendency: it is observable in several of the saints' figures in Novgorod.

In any case Rublev was already well over thirty by the time he joined Feofan's team, and presumably was well trained elsewhere; Moscow had teams of artists, even if not outstanding ones, by the mid-fourteenth century. No fewer than three teams

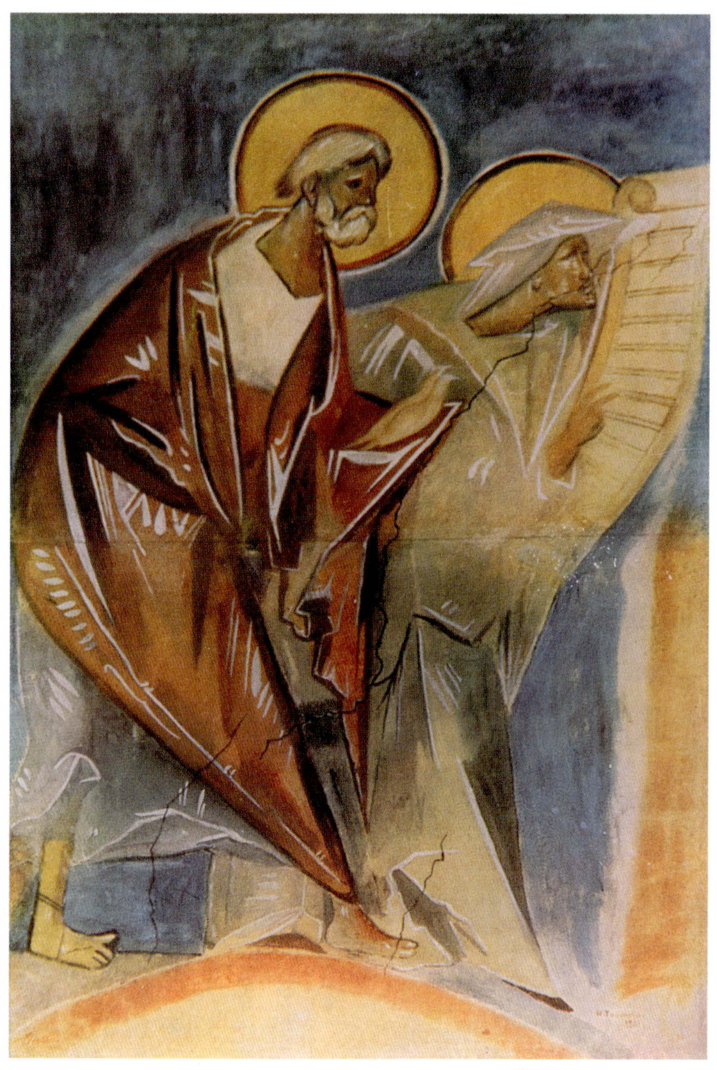

36 Joachim and Anna, from Presentation in the Temple, Volotovo, Novgorod. The fine local church of the Dormition at Volotovo was discovered to hold a remarkable set of frescoes of *c.* 1380 in the late 1930s; soon afterwards (1941) the building was reduced to rubble in the war, with only inadequate photographs and some coloured copies to preserve its memory, though slow restoration work has been undertaken. For Alpatov, this shows a Russification of Feofan's manner.

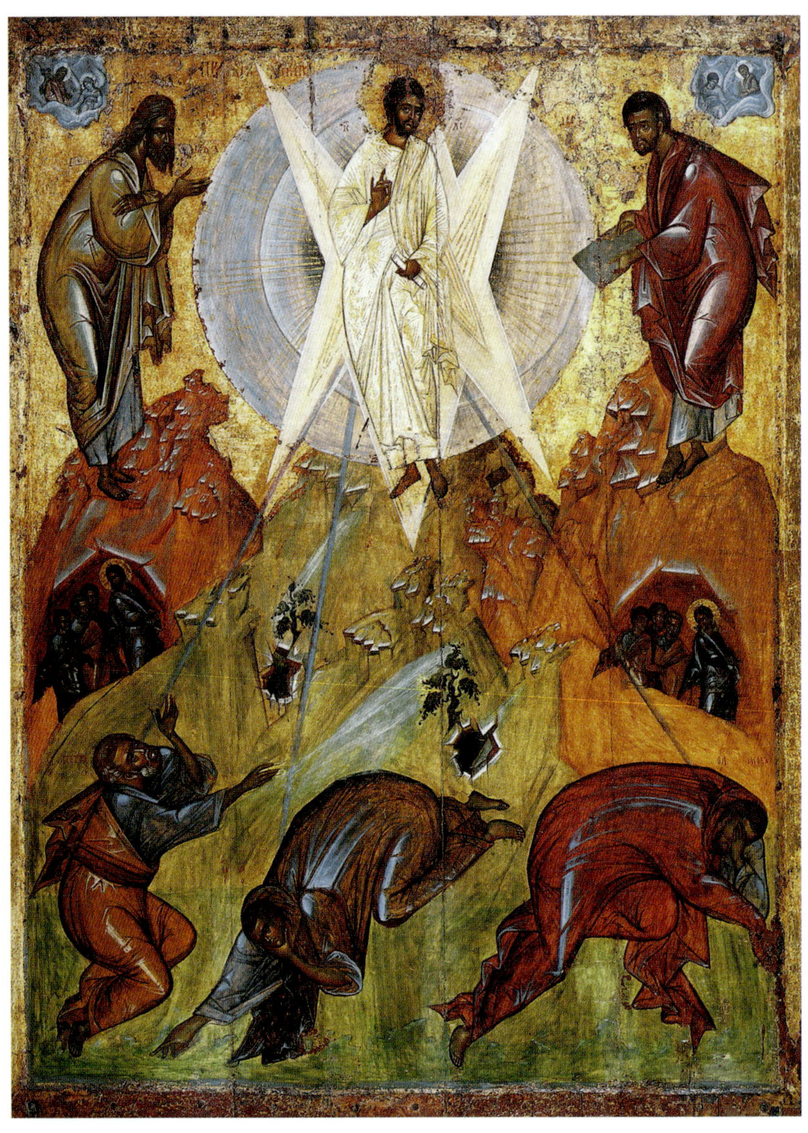

37 Feofan Grek or follower, a dramatic icon of the *Transfiguration*, late 14th century, from the Cathedral of the Transfiguration of the Saviour (1152–7) in the small appanage city of Pereslavl-Zalessky, northeast of Moscow.

were working in Moscow in the 1340s, one (identified as Goytan, Semyon and Ivan) described by the chronicler as 'Russians by birth, Greeks by training', indicating painters might study abroad. Clearly there was no language difficulty – nor was there with Feofan, who must have learnt Russian.

The term 'Hesychasm' deserves a further note. Literally 'Quietism', it was a mystical tendency, deriving from the Church Fathers, approved (after keen debate) as Orthodox doctrine in 1351. Its major proponent was St Gregory Palamas, a notable Athonite scholar. It involved silent contemplation and recital of the short 'Jesus prayer', and the possibility of an individual's accession to God's energies in the form of divine light. How it affected the practice of Orthodox religious life is a moot point, but it is evident that St Sergius was a strong adherent of the doctrine, and there are miracles in his 'Life' that seem to point in that direction: notably the appearance to him of the Mother of God in a blazing light, with a tree full of birds (his disciples).

The effects on Orthodox art are contentious: strong emotionalism, brilliant highlights (Feofan) and an immersive glow (Rublev) have been cited (illus. 37). Anita Strezova gives an exhaustive account, with a long chapter on Rublev – unfortunately not accurate enough to commend.[18] Positivistic historians (as Viktor Lazarev) tend to dismiss Hesychasm as disastrously retrograde. Beyond the Hesychast debate, the Orthodox Church in Russia seems to have avoided the sort of dissension that characterized the Western Church in the fourteenth century, save for the minor heresy of the 'Strigolniki' in Novgorod and Pskov, whose name, 'Shearers', remains mysterious and whose precepts are scarcely known, though seem to have been anti-clerical.

What would an apprentice painter have had to learn? First, to make icons, for which there was far more demand than for wall paintings. He would have to choose suitably seasoned boards (in Russia, preferably of lime; in Byzantium, of cypress), plane

them with a surface depression, strengthen them with dowels
at the back, find or make glues, fit a cloth to them, mix a series
of plasters to apply sequentially, then acquire, grind and mix the
right pigments (mostly earth colours, but probably also rarer
ones, and maybe gold leaf) from which to make egg tempera;
only then would he select and paint the proper iconographic
type – maybe using pattern books, though no such texts from
that period have survived – and brighten it all up with a varnish
of linseed oil, which would eventually darken. Colours would
be put on in layers, from dark to light, allowing fine tonal grad-
ation. The same would apply to wall paintings, where the paint,
in lime-wash, would have to be applied with considerable speed,
freehand, on wooden scaffolding, in a single short season – this
implied fresco technique, though it might be touched up in
secco. Complicated inscriptions would have to be accurately
rendered, and perspective distortions corrected. Rublev would
have had to go through all this, and at some point, doubtless in
the 1380s or '90s, he would have joined a team to learn wall
painting as an apprentice; clearly he did well.

At this point it is appropriate to investigate Rublev's special qualities more closely, but before that we should sketch
out the new and significant approach to the subject that has
emerged since circa 2015, as mentioned in Chapter Four. This
is bound up with the development over some decades of powerful and up-to-date technical equipment at the State Institute
of Restoration in Moscow (high-resolution microscopes, infra-
red and ultraviolet photography and so on). Such technology
permits the researcher a minute examination of the paintwork
and thus the opportunity to identify the individual brushstrokes
and layers, as well as the quantity of individual pigments in
any mixture. As far as Zvenigorod is concerned, at the time of
writing, the results seem only to have been published rather
obscurely in four articles by V. V. Baranov (one with colleagues),

deriving from conference papers, all in a single number of a Zvenigorod journal, though a book is promised.[19] Baranov progresses from his examination of the 'base' of the painting to the more evidently obvious details, thus in effect reversing the usual process by which the specialist would first assess the finished appearance of a painting and compare it with others, before, perhaps, investigating its more minute technicalities. Employing these methods, he shows convincingly that 1) in the Zvenigorod Range, the icons of St Michael and St Paul seem to be from the hand of one, very accomplished, painter; 2) the icon of Christ is by an even more skilled and self-assured painter, probably the leader of the team; 3) the *Old Testament Trinity* icon, for all its superficial similarities, is less assured in its underdrawing and realization, and comes from a different hand. He concludes that the attribution of the Zvenigorod icons to Rublev is mistaken.

The lengthy research and conclusions by Baranov and his colleagues hinge on a principle that he himself calls axiomatic: from the outset, an Old Russian painter would employ certain basic techniques or 'tricks of the trade' in mixing and applying undercoats, choosing pigments and so on; whatever the final result, these preparations would not vary – thus modern laboratory techniques can pinpoint a given artist and discover his 'handwriting' for the length of his career. Brilliant as the application of modern technological methods to icon painting certainly is, however, here the non-specialist may well raise an eyebrow. Quite how large a database do Baranov and colleagues have at their disposal where the icons of Rublev's time and earlier are concerned? The rather small number that survive are unsigned and usually undated (even the *Old Testament Trinity*). From the Zvenigorod range to the Trinity, more than twenty years probably elapsed. How can it be maintained, as a matter of faith, that Rublev's manner remained unaltered – into old age, in haste (as we know from Pakhomiy), in different circumstances, with different assistants, for a different purpose? It strains credulity. Baranov's metaphor of 'handwriting' reminds us that – while remaining recognizable – such an identifier can, and no doubt will, change over the course of a lifetime.

Baranov has a candidate for the leader of the team that painted Zvenigorod: Semyon Chorniy, who was deputy to Feofan the Greek in 1395 but unmentioned in his 1399 commission – both in Moscow. We have no surviving works by Semyon, so this is guesswork, but plausible, since he could hardly have been working in two places at once. If Semyon was team leader, however, and produced the icon of Christ, then there was a number two who made the Archangel and St Paul icons. The young Rublev would seem to fit the role well.

So let us turn to the three great surviving icons from Zvenigorod: they demonstrate the painter whom I still take to be Rublev, already well into his thirties, at the height of his powers. Given that much of the paintwork in each is completely missing, it is little short of miraculous that the paint surface, where it still exists, is in better condition than almost anywhere else in Rublev's oeuvre, letting one experience in particular the full impact of his talents as a colourist: the brilliant splash of ultramarine that energizes the saint and angel, the glowing red of the latter's garment.

What is more, the three icons of Christ, the Archangel Michael and St Paul let us sample three facets of sacred portraiture. The image of Christ, apparently understated, is in its way the most surprising: small-featured, grave yet unthreatening, like a well-meaning schoolmaster – as remote as possible from the famous fourteenth-century Moscow image of the 'Saviour of the Fierce Eye' (illus. 38), let alone Feofan's Pantocrator (see illus. 33). The indomitable St Paul is by contrast forcefully represented, but close to figures in the Vladimir paintings, particularly the folds of his garments, with their virtuoso cool colour effects.

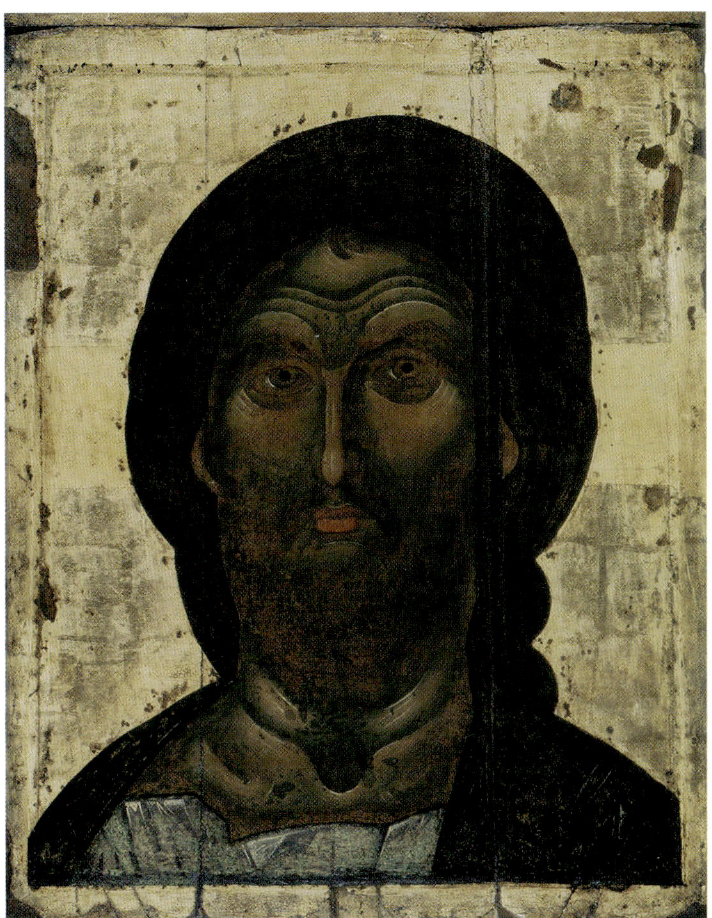

38 Saviour of the 'Fierce Eye' (*Spas yaroye oko*), Moscow, 14th century.
This weird and provincial, if unforgettable, icon was kept in the Kremlin
Dormition Cathedral, and would have been familiar to the young
Rublev, whose own versions of the Saviour are very different.

The Archangel shows the drama of St Michael's role as protector
of the Christian world not through any warrior-like gesture, but
through the dazzling use of red and ultramarine blue (red, incidentally, is by long tradition the symbolic colour of Russia itself).

This was a commission of high prestige; G. H. Hamilton aptly
notes 'the combination of intense aristocratic dignity with an

air of gentleness and compassion' as characteristically Russian.[20] We also notice the characteristic Rublevian angelic figure – almost his calling card – neither male nor female, old nor young, with a mass of tight curls (worthy of Leonardo da Vinci!) atop the rounded, inclined head. Its delicacy contrasts with the powerful St Michael icon that survives from Feofan and his team's painting of the first Archangel Cathedral in 1399 (see illus. 7).

We can move from St Michael to the other work of circa 1400 reasonably attributed to Rublev: the illustrations to the Khitrovo gospels. There were several high-quality gospel books produced around that time in Moscow. They are very similar, but in all commentators' opinion the Khitrovo is the finest. The image of an angel, beautifully set in a round frame (delicately impinged upon by his foot and halo), bears a strong resemblance to the Zvenigorod archangel, though with magnificently rendered garments, in cool shaded blues, similar to St Paul's (see illus. 31). No less memorable is the somewhat dove-like eagle representing St John, its tail just interrupting the circle. One can reasonably sense a certain playfulness here – as also in the charmingly weird initial capitals displaying fabulous beasts; these of course are not limited to the Khitrovo book, but treated here less solemnly and more confidently than elsewhere, their spirit rather surprisingly like that of certain minor figures in the Vladimir *Last Judgement* scenes (see illus. 30). The picture of St John and Prochoros on Patmos is nicely framed by fancifully tottering mountains (see illus. 25).

The Vladimir wall paintings – largely an elaborate *Last Judgement* cycle – are the only ones by Rublev to have survived (with the exception of small fragments, found as underfloor rubble), and are in poor condition (illus. 40, 41, 42, 43). They are also not attributable wholly to him, since Daniil was his collaborator on the scheme. To separate their work is impossible, for lack of anything else by Daniil for comparison, though some scenes (notably Abraham's Bosom) display a rather archaic manner that would fit with earlier fourteenth-century art, by an older man (illus. 39). Overall they make a magnificent ensemble – for Viktor Lazarev 'architectonic' in the best sense, giving meaning to the vaults and columns of the nave (illus. 44).[21]

In several scenes Rublev's gift for the dynamic grouping of figures is manifest (illus. 45); everywhere the terrifying threat of judgement is mitigated by the expectant, awestruck expressiveness of the simply yet movingly delineated facial types – Russian, rather than Byzantine (illus. 46). This point becomes abundantly clear if one takes a short walk to the late twelfth-century St Demetrius Cathedral, which boasts, as luck would have it, a similar seated group of apostles and angelic warriors, in lively conversation, doubtless painted by a Greek two hundred years earlier. Rublev must have known this rather different

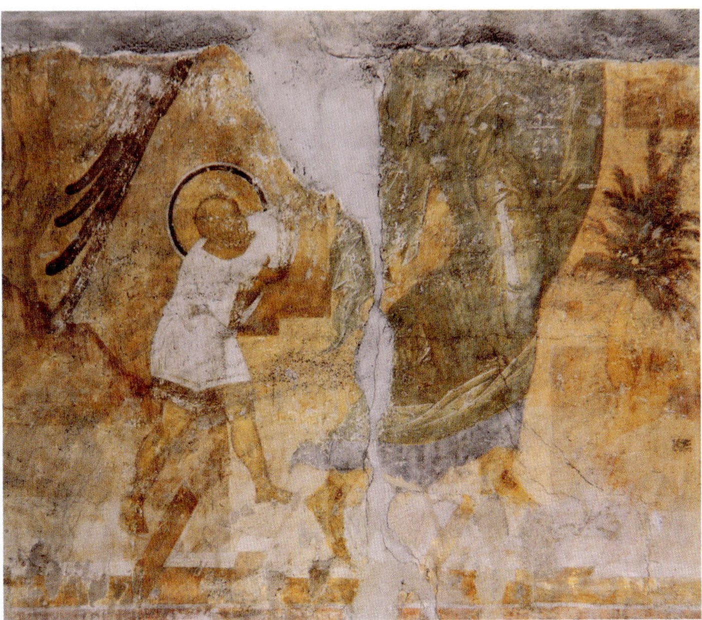

39 Vladimir Dormition (attrib. to Daniil): John the Baptist as a child, led by an angel.

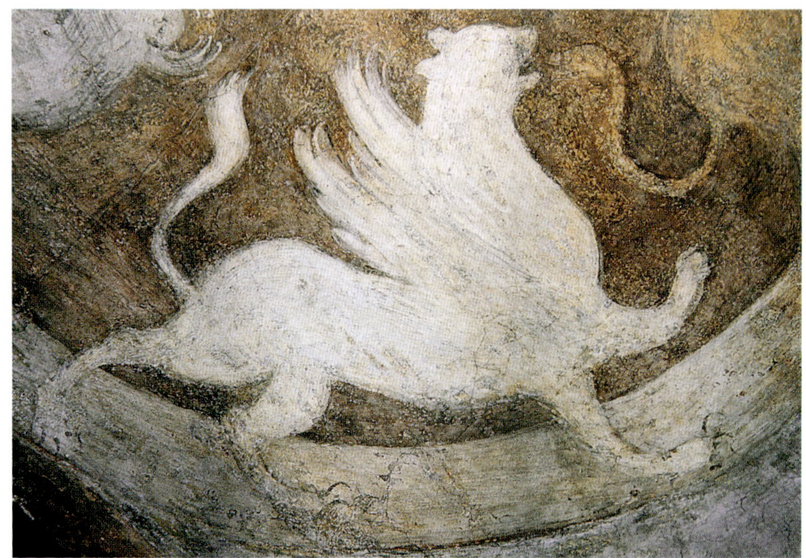

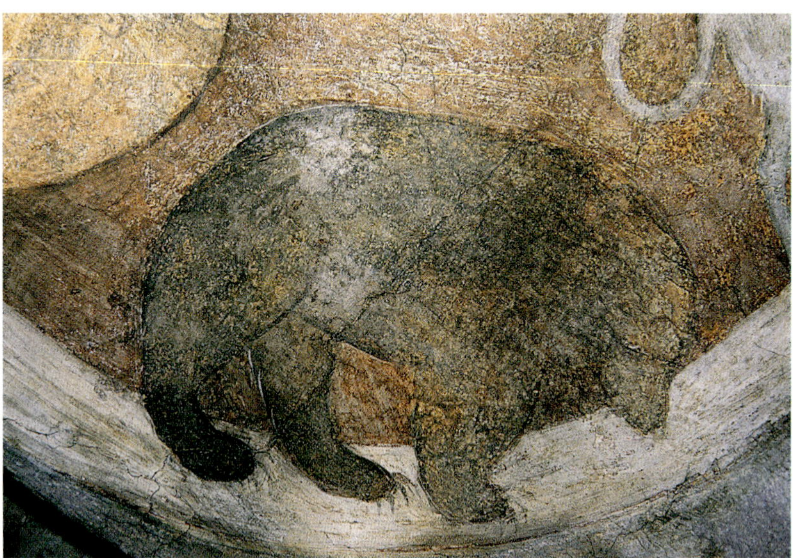

40, 41, 42, 43 Vladimir Dormition: the four beasts of the prophet
Daniel's vision, 'diverse from one another' (Daniel 7:2–17), represent
empires of antiquity: the Babylonian, Macedonian, Roman and that
of Antichrist, 'dreadful and terrible . . . diverse from all the beasts that

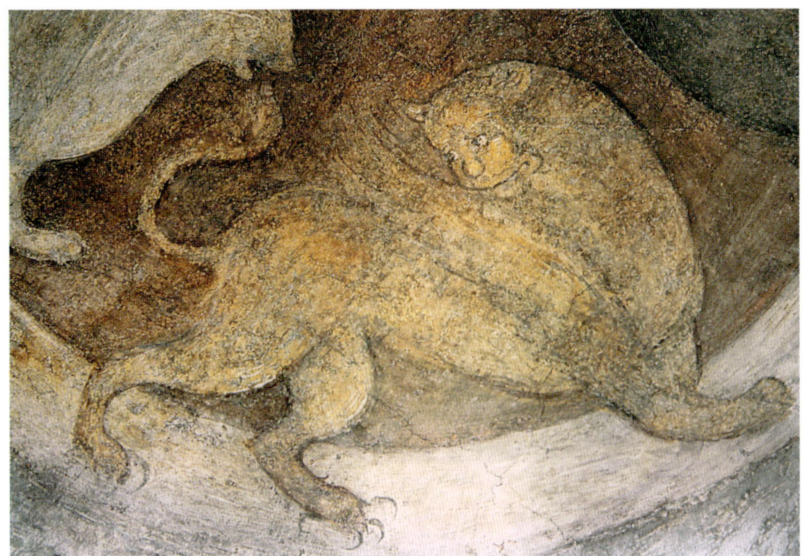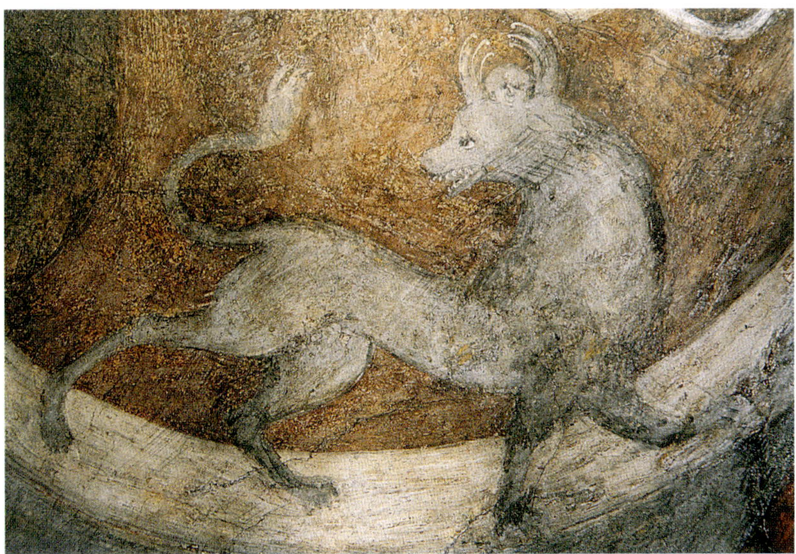

were before it'. To medieval thinkers, up-to-date realms could replace them, with the bear representing Russia and the fourth beast perhaps the Tatars. The beasts (particularly the bear) seem rather more playful than savage here.

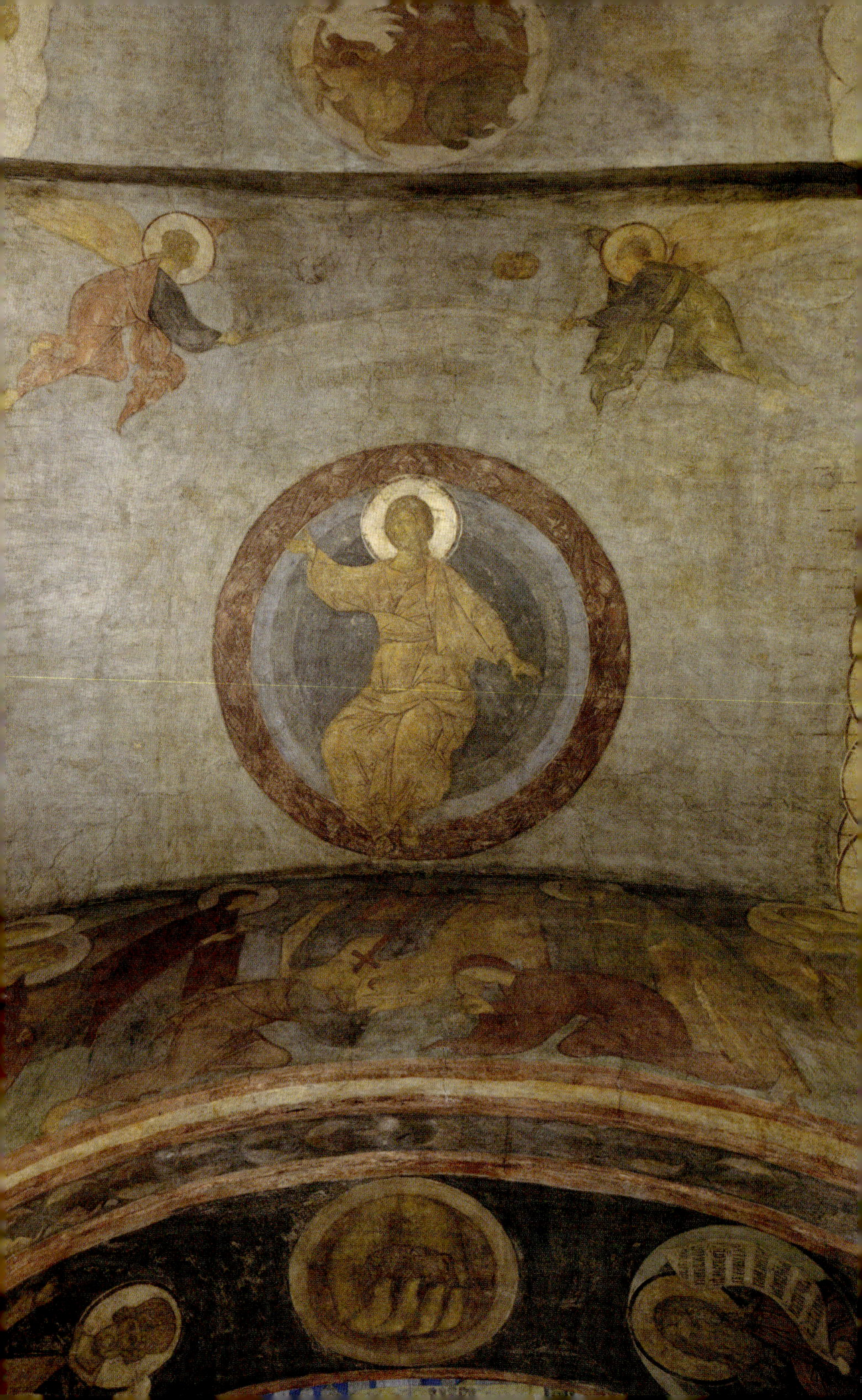

    Rublev as Artist

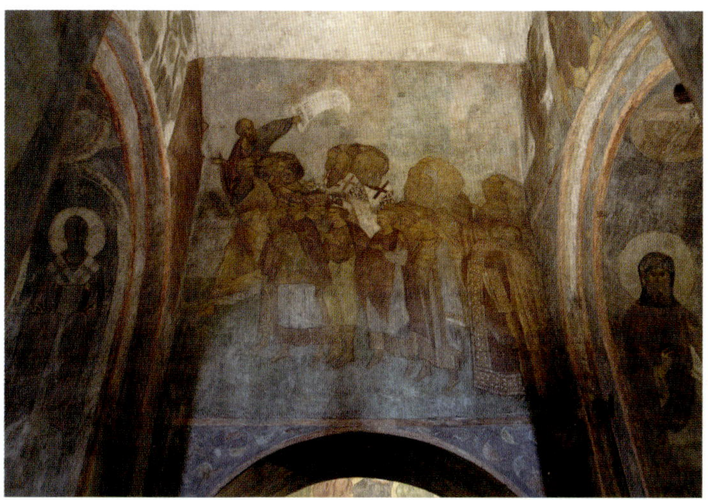

45 Vladimir Dormition: Entry of the Righteous Men into Paradise.
With a sweeping gesture St Paul ushers forward the awestruck figures of
the Righteous (Apostles to the fore, bishops behind them, royalty below).

Last Judgement and distanced himself from its spirit and its facial
types. There are several rather whimsical details, now very hard
to discern, in the overall scheme: notably the elegant trumpet-
ing angels, and the figures in the *Earth and the Sea Yield Their
Dead* (illus. 47).

All such details, and the wonderful Khitrovo illustrations,
add to the realization that Rublev (when he has the opportunity) is a superb, imaginative draftsman (illus. 48). But in this
connection an important point needs to be made. Iconic images
are often thought of as two-dimensional, 'flattened', with un-
modulated, full-face figures. Such, particularly in a folk context,
they might become, and maybe were beginning to become in

44 Christ in Glory, commanding the Last Judgement to begin: centrepiece of western bays of nave in the Vladimir Dormition Cathedral,
Daniil and Rublev, 1408, fresco. Above this: roundel containing the four
beasts of the Prophet Daniel's vision (Daniel 7). Below: Adam and Eve,
and roundel containing 'the souls of the righteous in God's hand'.

Dionisiy's time. However, a glance at any of Rublev's authentic works shows how questionable this idea can be. Byzantine art seldom uses true shadows, which imply a definite light source. Rather, the careful build-up of tone from dark to light, in faces or garments, permits a satisfying three-dimensionality devoid of ostentation, entirely in accord with the spirit of antiquity (illus. 49).

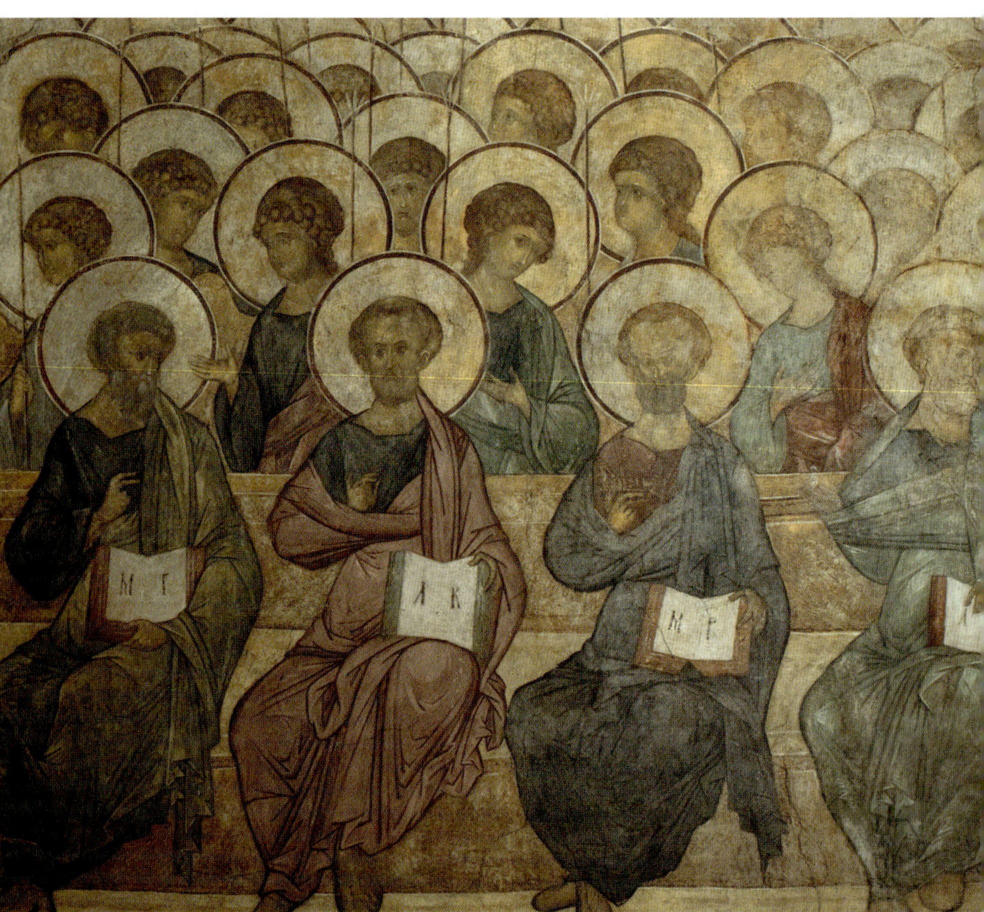

46 Vladimir Dormition: rows of seated Apostles (no two identical), with angels behind; relatively well-preserved. (L–R): Matthew, Luke, Mark and Andrew.

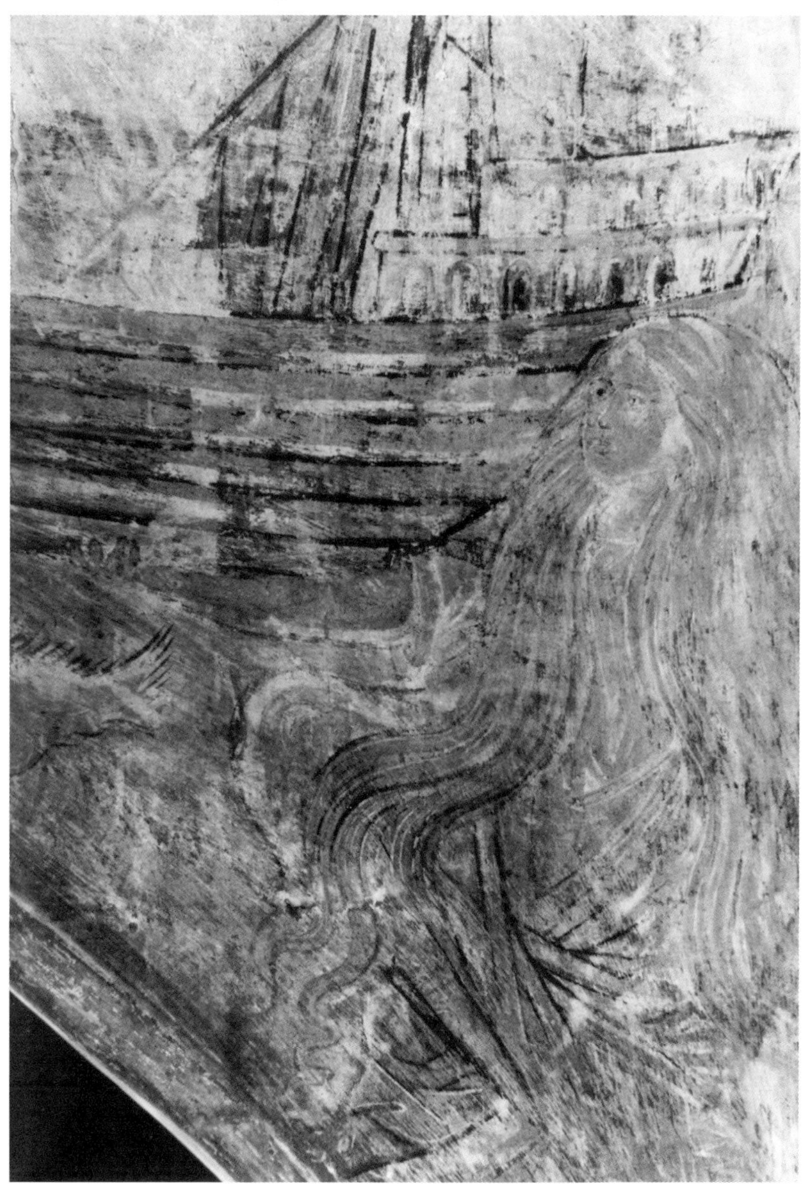

47 Vladimir Dormition: 'the Earth and the Sea Yield up their Dead' (detail). Particularly hard to make out from ground level, this scene displays great graphic virtuosity; note the shipwreck below the personification of the Sea, with her remarkable hair style.

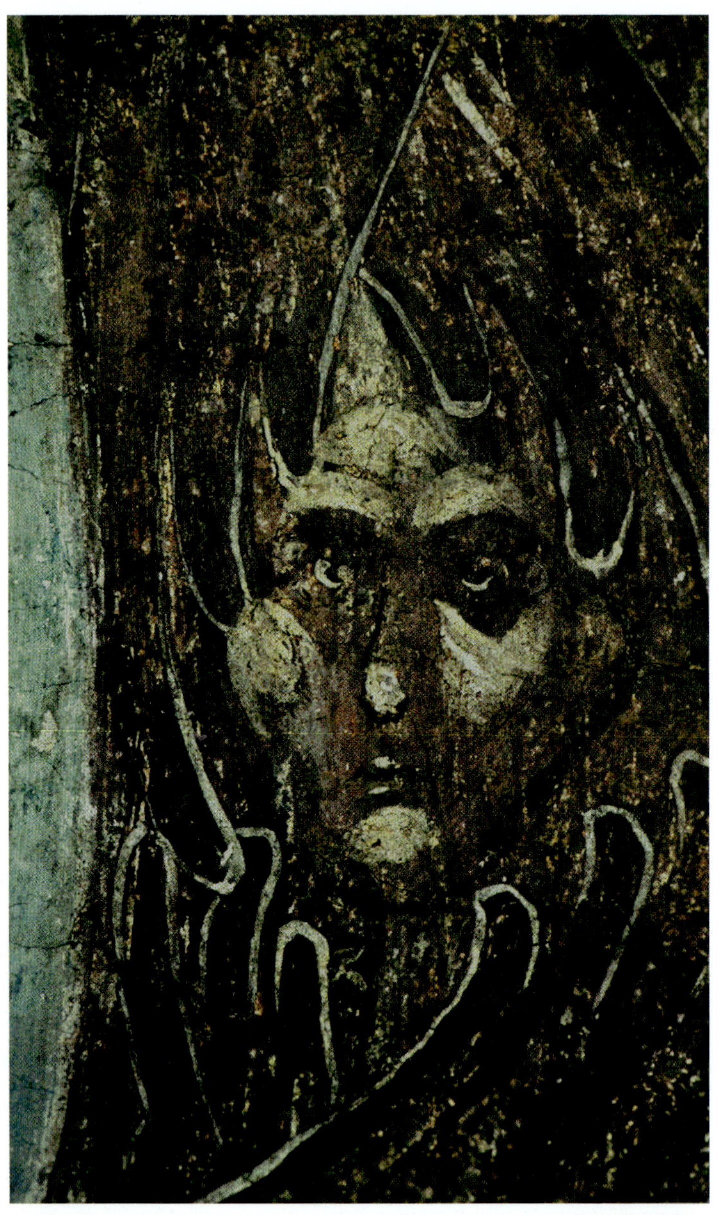

48 Vladimir Dormition: seraph, one of those surrounding Christ in the central roundel.

49 Vladimir Dormition: Entry of the Goodly Women and Martyrs into Paradise. The holy women, in elegant headdresses, form a remarkable close group.

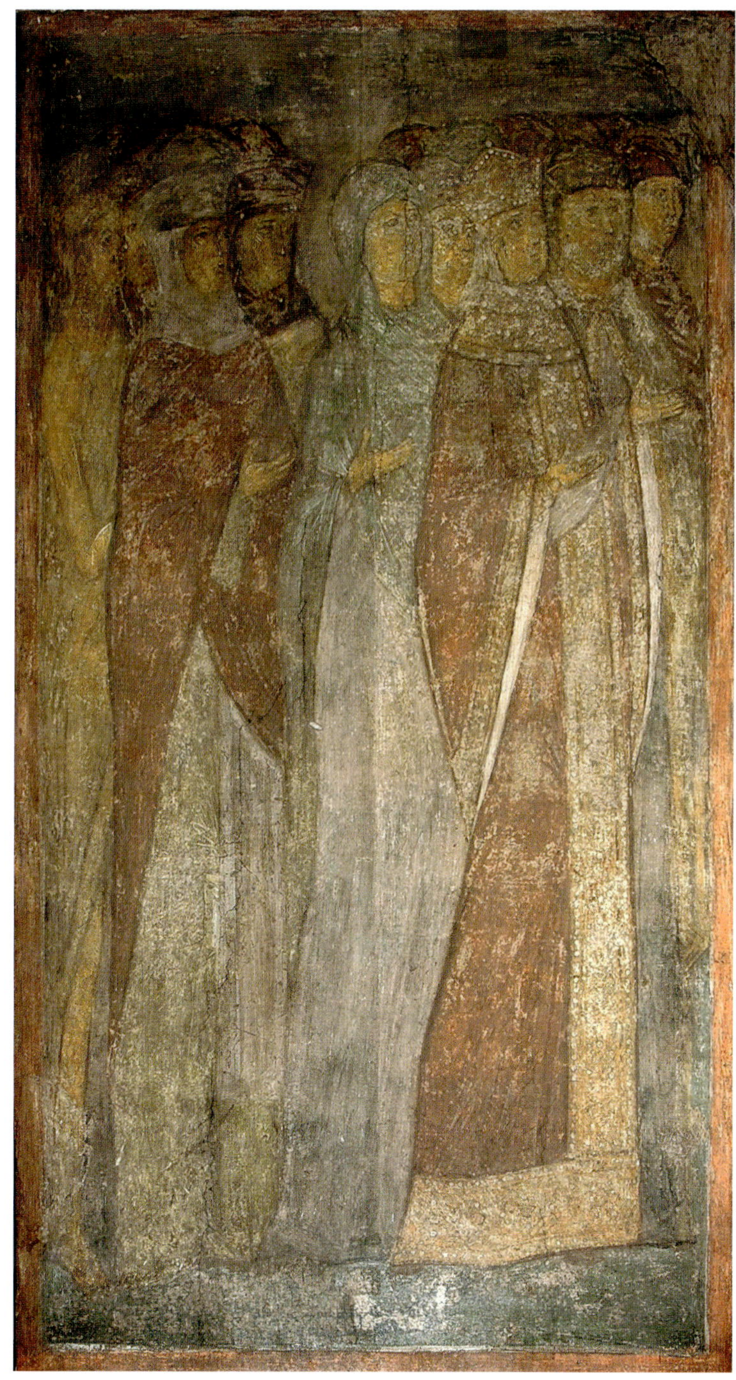

Larger figures of Rublev's time stand with more than a hint of contrapposto, their heads usually bowed and viewed three-quarter face. A final but significant point needs to be made: while scenes of the torments of sinners in hell – familiar in the West – are not entirely lacking in Orthodox art, it is far more orientated towards the ecstatic elements of Judgement Day (as described, for example, in 1 Thessalonians 4 and 1 Corinthians 15). This may be down to what – by chance – has survived, but there are no torments in the Vladimir frescoes, and plenty that is ecstatic.

As for the surviving icons, the main ones over 3 metres high, from the great Vladimiriconostasis, they present a problem: one can envisage Rublev and/or Daniil as having sketched out their general lines for assistants to fill in (illus. 50, 51). The same could be said about the largest early iconostasis in situ, at the Trinity Monastery – in considerable need of proper conservation, incidentally (see illus. 20). But the jewel of this iconostasis, and no doubt the intended summit of Rublev's career, was of course the legendary icon of the *Hospitality of Abraham* or *Old Testament Trinity* that held pride of place in the local (lowest) tier for some five hundred years.

In that time it got quite a battering, as anyone who looks at it closely will see. The paint surface, particularly on the garment of the left-hand angel, is worn. The tree of Mamre survived only in fragments, and is now largely a later overpainting. The haloes have lost their gold leaf. The paintwork on the table is worn down to the gesso beneath. Tiny fragments of colour suggest there was something originally on top: triangular pieces of bread have been proposed. There may have been some touching up of the faces. The upper surface is pitted with little holes, from the application of a silver casing in the mid-sixteenth century. There was much overpainting, to the initial disappointment of the first restorers to examine it (1904–5); they soon realized what a treasure they had laid their hands on, yet having cleaned

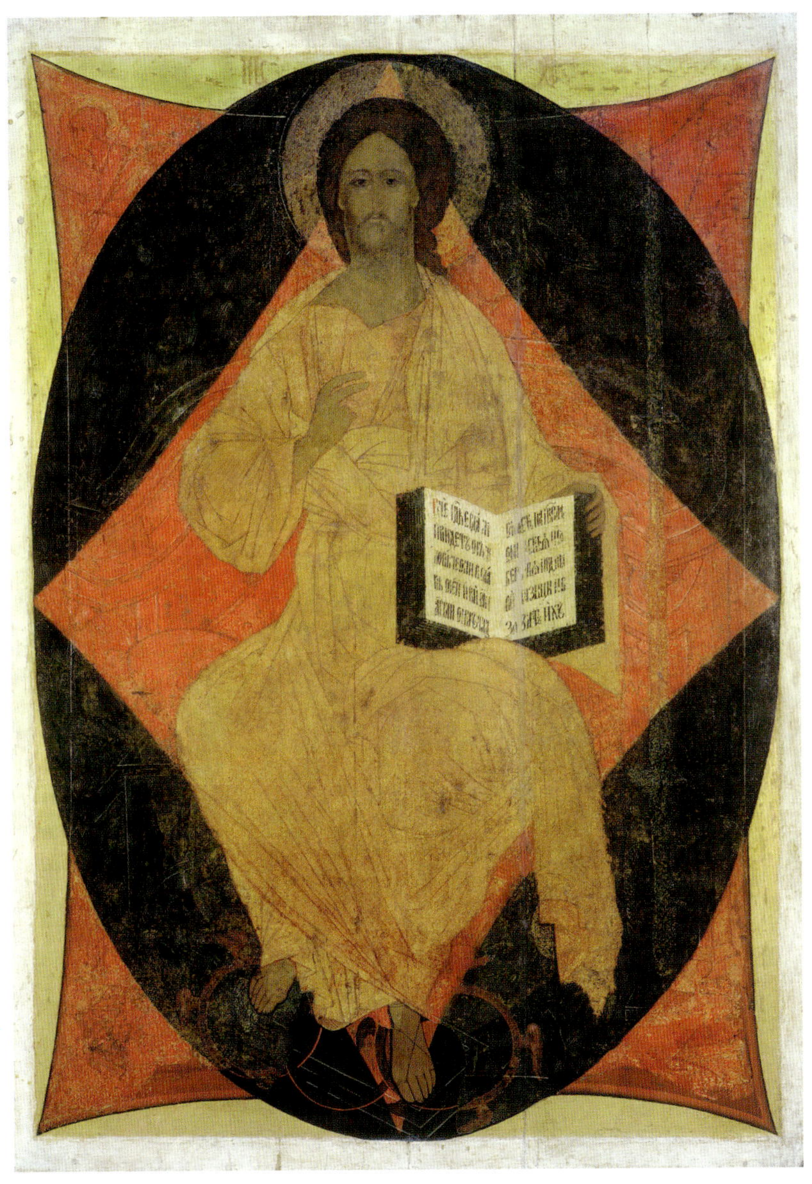

50 Vladimir Dormition, iconostasis: *Christ in Glory*. Such an icon is the centrepiece of any 'high' iconostasis. This very large one, much damaged in its time, was doubtless executed – if not planned – by assistants of Rublev and Daniil.

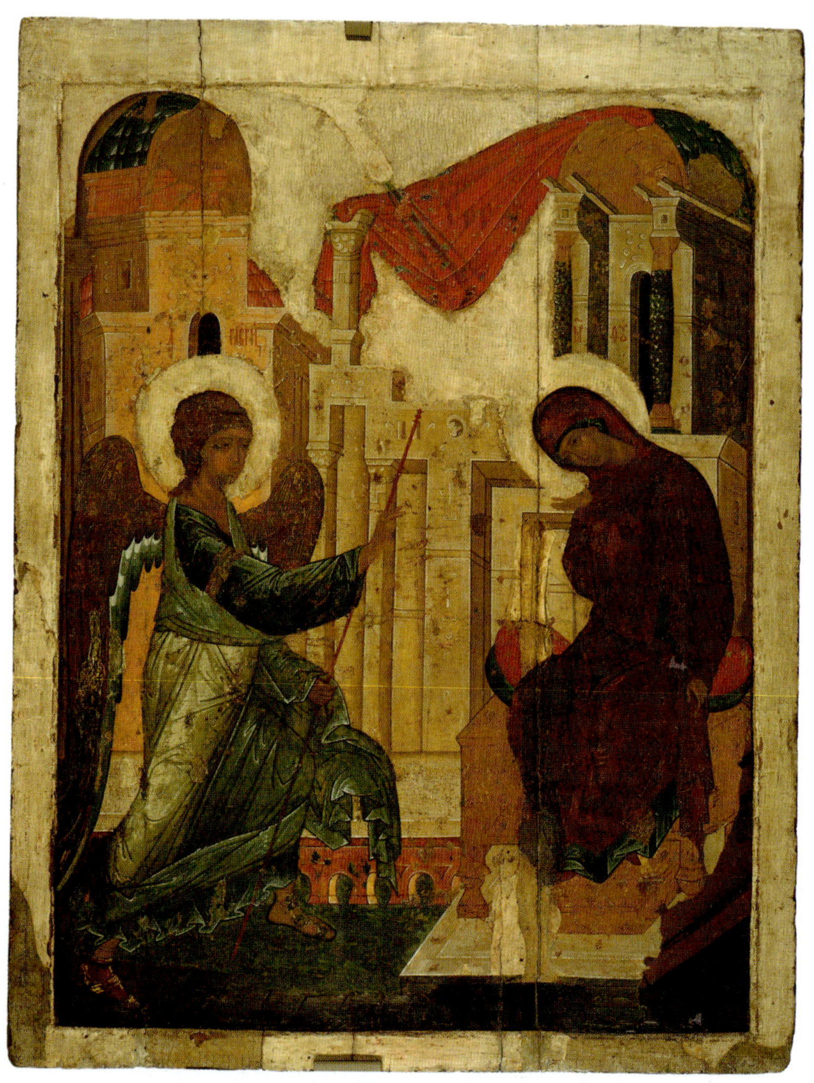

51 *Annunciation*, from the 'Feast Day' tier of Vladimir Dormition iconostasis. Three exceptionally fine icons survive from among the smaller icons sold in the 18th century – they suggest a greater input by Rublev or Daniil than do the Deisus icons.

it as well as they could, they replaced the casing (finally removed in 1919). Whole essays were written about Rublev on the basis of one black-and-white photograph. This at least demonstrates the power of the hypnotically circular composition, with three angelic figures silently conversing; the force of its colour effects (with the extraordinary central splash of ultramarine and red, leading inexorably to the sacrificial chalice) could wait for appreciation.

Forgive us, please, for revisiting some of the points made in Chapter One about this incredible picture – it is worth going over them again. The Hospitality of Abraham is an ancient iconic theme in Christian art; the slightly mysterious visit of three men to Abraham (Genesis 18) is of course taken symbolically to represent the Trinity – albeit arguments about the legitimacy of such a representation rumbled on.[22] Earlier versions are rather cluttered, showing Abraham and Sarah, and often, too, prepa-rations for the feast the men are to be offered. Only subsequently is their angelic nature understood. In early representations (as notably in S. Vitale, Ravenna) the three angels are rather awk-wardly seated side-by-side; later versions – particularly some Novgorod icons of around Rublev's time – have a more satisfac-tory composition, though with the central figure dominating the outer ones: see Feofan's notable version in the Transfiguration church on Ilyin Street (illus. 52).

This can inspire wrangling, ultimately futile, over which angel represents which person of the Trinity. Circular versions of the scene – on, for example, pilgrims' badges – led ultimately to Rublev's brilliant resolution of its problematic nature. It seems nevertheless that the central figure for him has the attributes of the Son, with the blood-red sleeve exactly repeated in the chal-ice (all that survives of the feast), which must signify sacrifice. To leave out Abraham and Sarah was an extraordinary move: they are seen only in their attributes, those indeed of all worldly

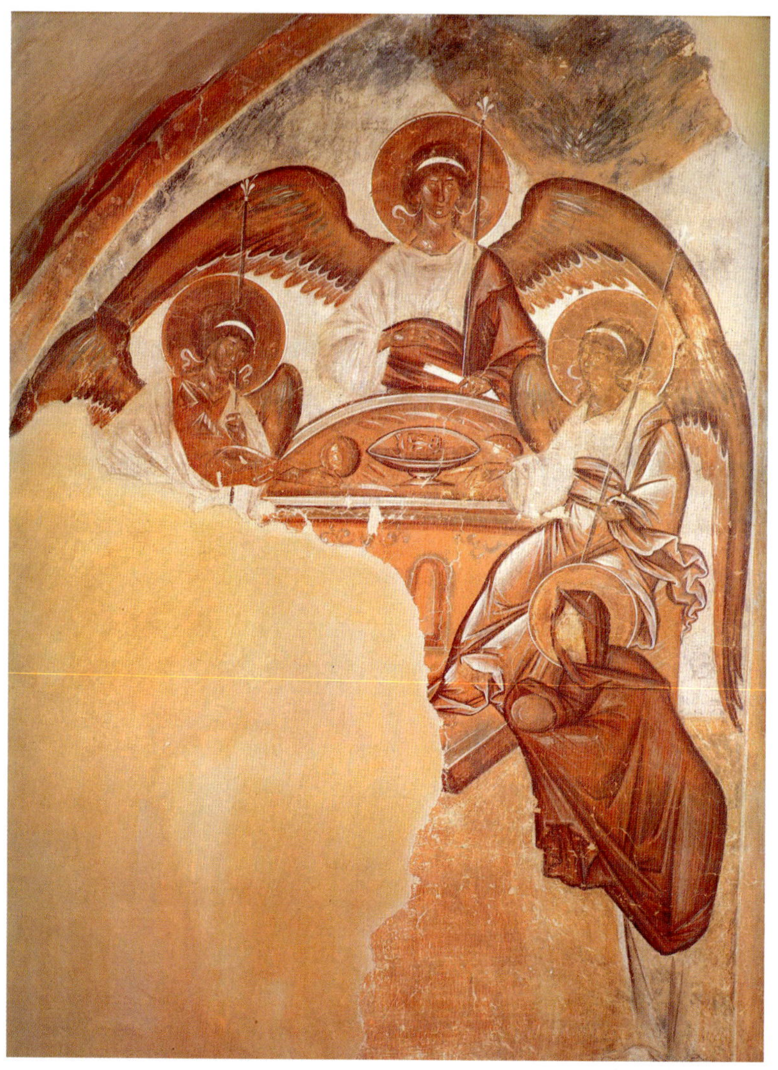

52 Feofan Grek, *Old Testament Trinity*, 1378, wall painting from
Church of the Transfiguration on Ilyin (that is, Elijah) Street,
Novgorod. This is the only certain surviving work from Feofan's
hand. The differences from Rublev's later Trinity icon are plain
to see: a curved table, the dominance of the central figure, the
clutter of the feast, the presence of Sarah, the ribbons (indicating
'listening') waving from each angel's head – all made more striking
by the brown-and-white chiaroscuro effect.

life: the house, the tree and the mountain (on which Abraham would come near to sacrificing Isaac). The angelic attributes by contrast are wand-like staves, reminding us that we are on a journey through the world.

We know from the seventeenth-century 'Tale of the Holy Icon Painters' that Rublev was commissioned by Nikon, Sergius's successor, to paint the icon in praise of Sergius and to counter the enmities of the world – unity-in-diversity has always been taken in Russia as the prime significance of the Trinity. Where it can have first stood is difficult to determine. The fierce raid by the Tatar commander Edigey in December 1408 (just after Andrey and Daniil had completed the Vladimir Dormition Cathedral, though probably not yet its icon-screen) burned the Trinity Monastery to ashes – see Yepifany's letter. A wooden church was constructed on its site: could Rublev have painted his great memorial-icon for this? More likely, one would have thought, it was made for its replacement in stone (illus. 53), which he and Daniil painted in the mid-1420s, shortly before Nikon's death (1427). The modern scholar Vladimir Plugin proposes that the *Trinity* was painted for Zvenigorod (though it is not of identical dimensions to the surviving icons of its range) and presented to the monastery by Ivan IV after 1547. The question is of minor importance, anyhow. We are left with a painting that, like many of the most inspired works of art, manages to be both simple and endlessly suggestive at the same time.

I believe there should be a coda to our brief account of Rublev as artist, relating to his final retreat, the Andronikov Monastery. It derives from Pakhomiy's account of the building of the cathedral at the monastery in the late 1420s: the abbot Alexander and a senior monk, Andrey, 'created an extremely beautiful church of stone, and decorated it with their own hands' (from the 'Life' of Nikon in the Second Sofia Chronicle, mid-fifteenth century; see illus. 22). The phrase, it seems to me, is unequivocal. Yet the art historians who have pored over every inch of Rublev's possible or actual paintings consistently ignore it, even though an architectural historian, P. N. Maksimov, raised the question of Rublev's authorship as long ago as the 1940s.

It is fair to note that the cathedral was in a dilapidated state until its careful restoration in 1959–60; by then the likes of Igor Grabar, Lazarev and Alpatov had no doubt finally formed their views. Valeriy Sergeyev does mention the possibility, but quickly slips away from it on the curious grounds that there is no evidence the abbot had any architectural skills. Yet such a major building, in a quite small monastery, could hardly be constructed without such discussion; Rublev was one of the senior monks, a *starets*, in Pakhomiy's words 'excelling all in his wisdom, with honourable grey hair'. To have the foremost artist of his time residing there must have been a singular honour for the brethren; what is more, the recently completed work by Daniil and Rublev at the Trinity Monastery could have brought in the considerable sum that such a stone building would have cost (illus. 54).

If Giotto could design the Florentine bell-tower, why should Rublev in consultation with the abbot not have designed the monastery cathedral as his last project? It is a building of remarkable grace and originality, of finely cut limestone blocks, its tiers of superposed ogees (*kokoshniki*) clambering upwards as if to reach for heaven, perhaps like a growing fir tree (it should be noted that slight pointing of basically Romanesque arches is

53 First stone church of the Trinity Monastery Cathedral, 1422/3, present view, replacing the wooden one built after Edigey's destructive raid of 1408 – the *Old Testament Trinity* icon may have been originally made for one or the other. Externally simple, but with the walls slightly canted inwards to increase its apparent height. Inside, St Sergius's tomb. The wall-painting, done hastily by Andrey, Daniil and their team, has been replaced, but the high iconostasis is the oldest to survive in situ.

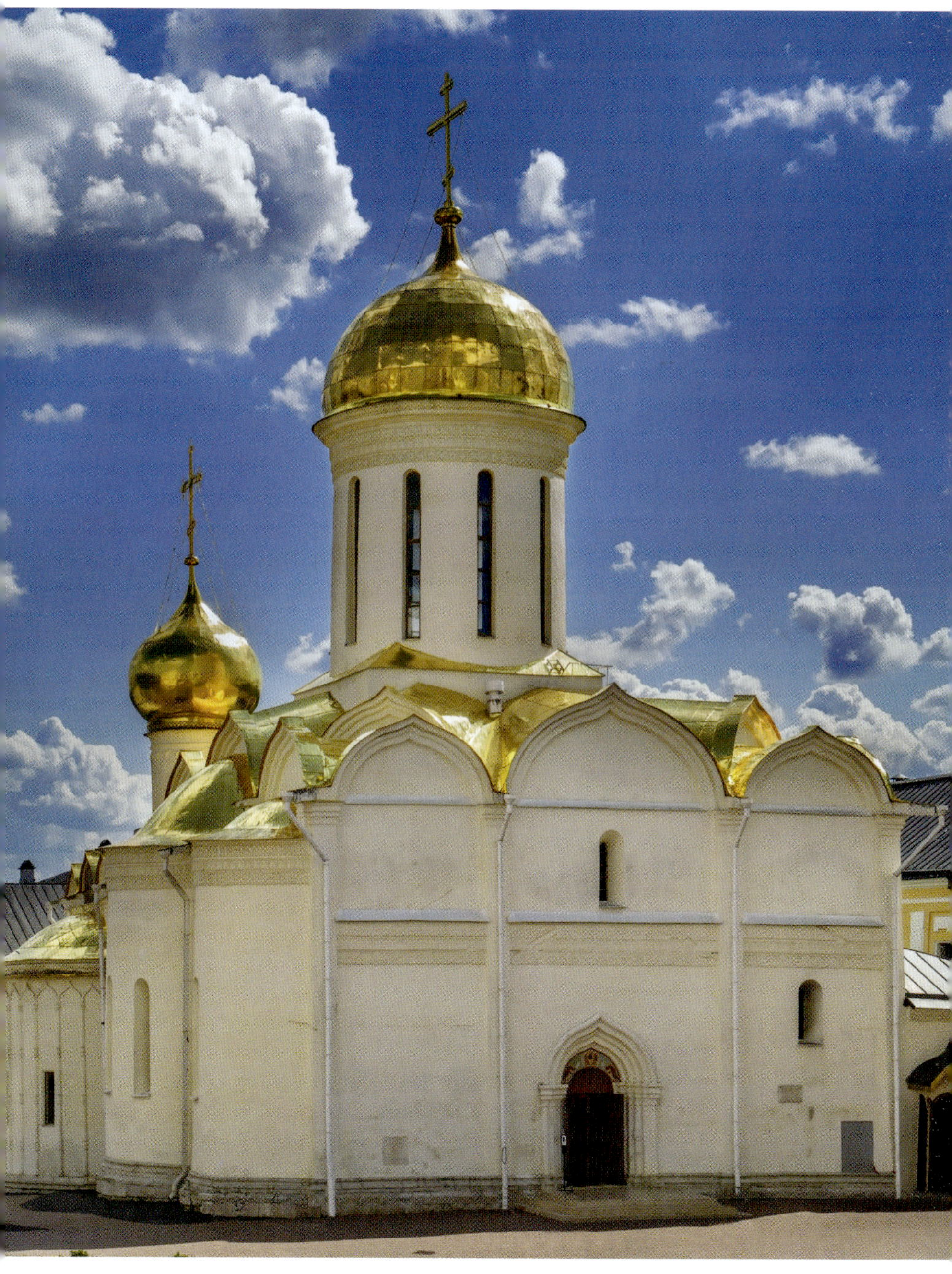

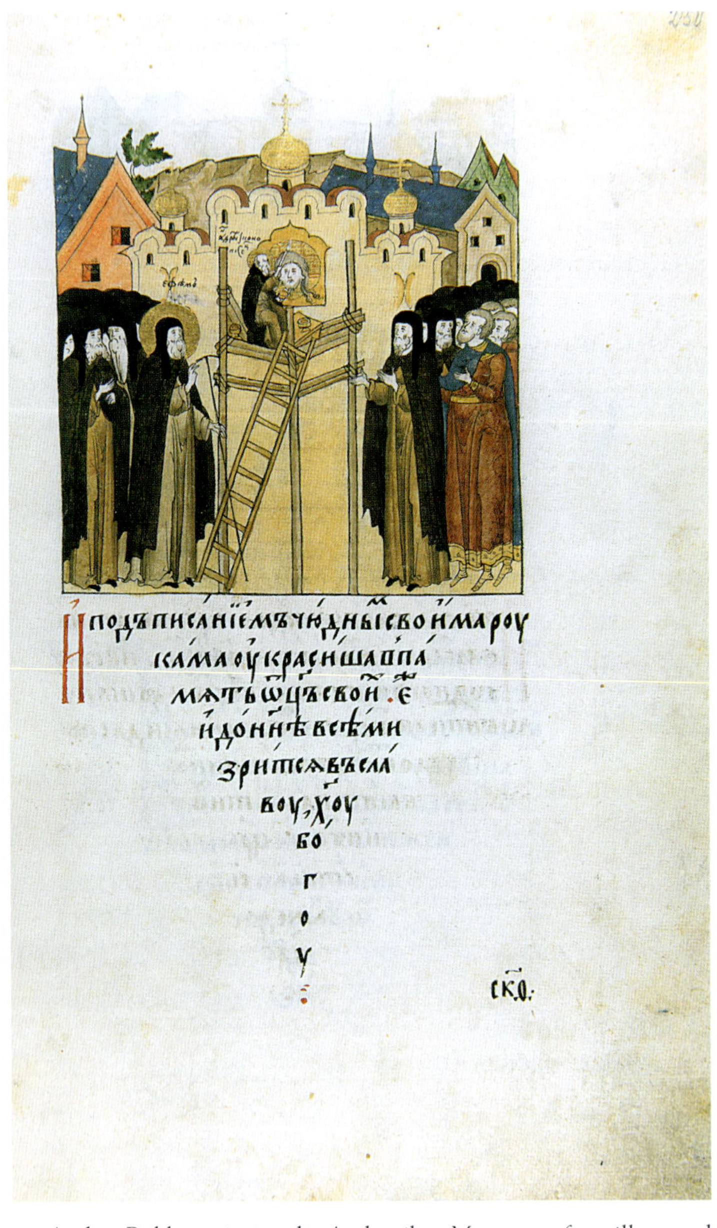

54 Andrey Rublev painting the Andronikov Monastery, from illustrated edition of *Life of St Sergius* (1580s–early 1590s). Characteristic stylized rendering of the period, featuring admiring monks and townsfolk.

observable in two late churches of Vladimir Rus, at Suzdal and Yuriev-Polskiy).

Actually it has a distinguished place in the history of architecture: it is the culminating work of the brief but highly interesting style of 'early Muscovite' building. How this originated is unknown: none of the usually suggested derivations, from churches in Galich in Ukraine, Chernigov, Novgorod or Vladimir, are more than fleetingly convincing, though in some we find a 'pyramidal' tendency – matched also in the superposed arches of the unusual Serbian church of Gračanica (1321). Masonry buildings were a fourteenth-century innovation in Moscow anyhow. The first Dormition cathedral of the Kremlin (1326), when its foundations were excavated, turned out to have the same ground-plan as St George at Yuriev-Polskiy (or Polskoy, 1230), the last of the great Vladimir churches, located quite near Moscow. The five surviving early Moscow buildings, however, are plain in plan, but externally remarkable. Ogee arches – later piled up rather indiscriminately in Russian buildings – make almost their first, rather mysterious and subtle appearance in these structures (they do not seem to relate to the pointed arches of contemporary Gothic style or styles). To quote a modern historian of architecture, 'The attempt was made here to create an entirely new form of church . . . an event of cardinal importance and novelty.'[23] Could Rublev not at least have sketched out its plan?

There is a further strange twist to the story. The other truly remarkable building of this style, a quarter-century earlier, is the small but very elegant cathedral of the Dormition in Zvenigorod, built under Prince Yuriy Dmitrievich circa 1399. It suffers now from having a flat roof imposed on it, though once it too sported *kokoshniki*. With its long, narrow engaged columns and its intricate ornamental frieze, it combines great elegance with exuberance. The exterior columns and internal

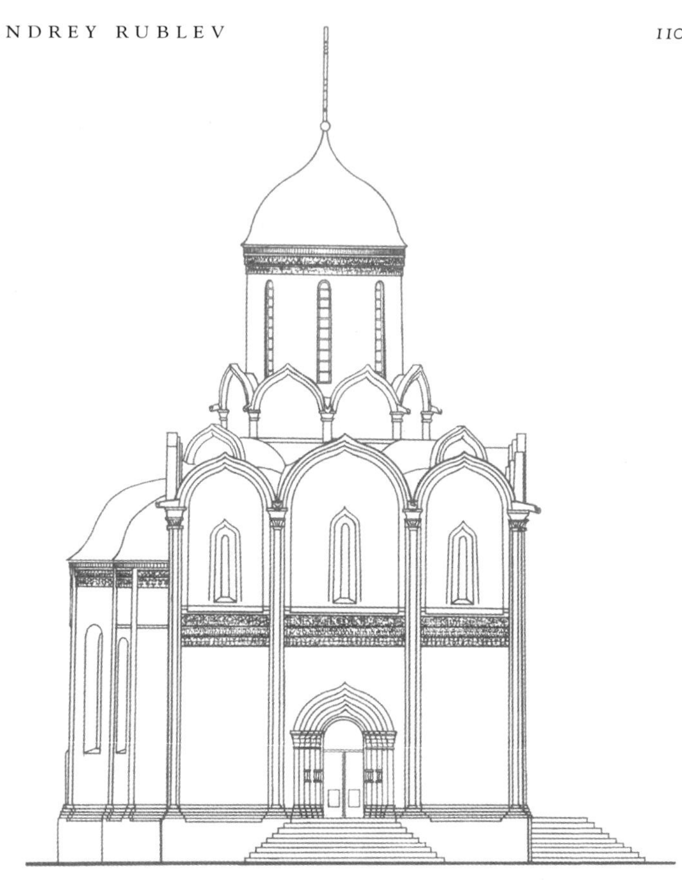

55 Proposed reconstruction of Dormition Cathedral in Zvenigorod,
c. 1399, by B. A. Ognyov (1955), showing appearance before later
changes; the elegant exterior columns are decorative features, not
corresponding to internal articulation.

piers no longer correspond – this is in conception a 'painterly'
work (illus. 55, 56). With reference to it, the architectural historian Dmitriy Shvidkovsky cites both St Sergius and Rublev:
'to the culture represented by these two men, the cathedral in
Zvenigorod, so rich and subtle in all its traditional simplicity,
must surely be said to belong.'[24]

But as it happens this is just the time at which Rublev is
thought to have painted the incomparable Zvenigorod range

of icons for the same prince and for the same church. It may be excessively speculative, but I suggest he had a hand in its design, too. After Rublev's and Yuriy's time, it should be noted, Yuriy's sons engaged in a long dynastic struggle, if not a civil war, for the throne of Moscow, and for 25 years (1425–50), masonry building in Moscow lapsed. Later, just a few buildings (such as

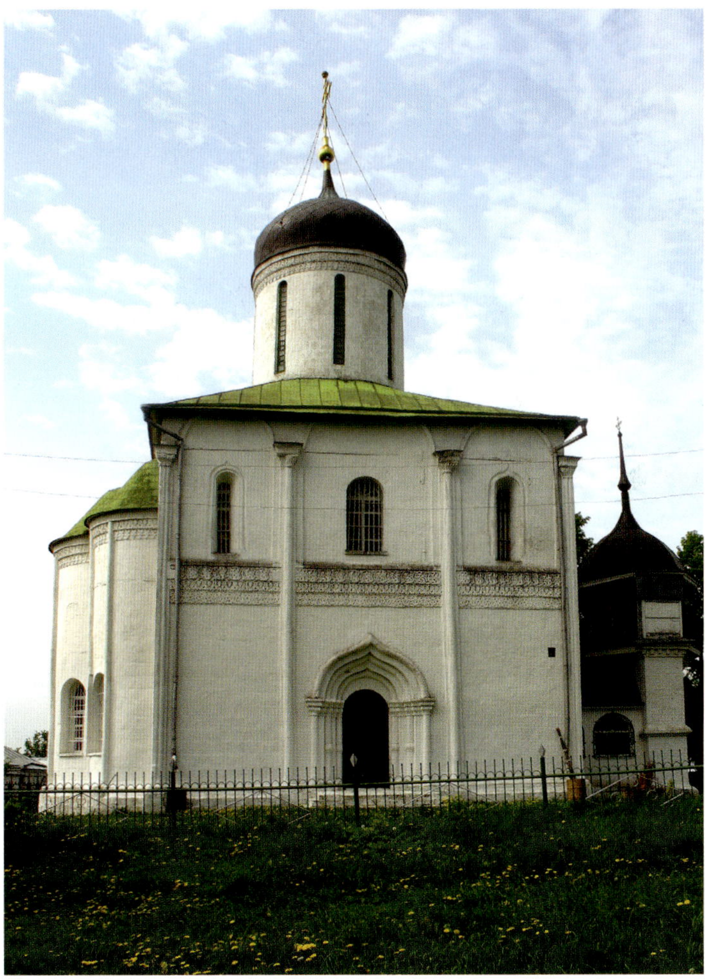

56 Dormition Cathedral 'on the Hill', Zvenigorod, *c.* 1399, present view, showing flat roof.

the Kremlin Annunciation Cathedral, 1480s, and the Knyaginin convent, Vladimir, end of the fifteenth century) picked the style up more or less convincingly, only for many later buildings to be drowned in an excess of *kokoshniki*.

SIX

Afterwards

In the eighteenth century Russian art thoroughly absorbed Western European principles and methods. Or rather, art on any sophisticated level did; folk art of various kinds continued to thrive, and with it icon painting, though normally of a humble sort, disregarded by cognoscenti. Icon painting was also inextricably entangled with the Church, whose deficiencies on several levels were all too apparent to the intellectual class.

In 1828 the author Prince Vyazemsky could write a long poem mocking the 'Russian God' ('Full of grace to the stupid,/ Mercilessly strict to the clever,/ God of everything inappropriate,/ That is him, the Russian God . . .'), yet by mid-century the mood had shifted, Orthodoxy began to be valued by intellectuals, and historical societies arose. The most successful of these, the Moscow Antiquarian Society (founded in 1864), was instrumental in first revealing the Vladimir Dormition frescoes (1882). The Dormition iconostasis, sold to the parishioners of the Trinity Church in the village of Vasilevskoye, was actually cleaned in the 1850s, but caused no great stir then or for many years to come. But things were on the move. Self-renewal in the Church, and the encouragement of successive tsars, helped; so indeed did literary works, particularly N. Leskov's tale 'The Sealed Angel' (1872). Unfortunately, early cleaning methods, kept a close secret by the practitioners, could be crude and indeed damaging.

The name of Rublev was not, of course, forgotten – the injunction by the 'Council of 100 Chapters' ('Stoglav', 1551) to paint like him and the Greek masters was famous; the first general historian of Russia, Nikolay Karamzin, had read the Trinity Chronicle before the 1812 fire, and knew of Rublev's 1405 and 1408 commissions. Part of the trouble in the eighteenth and nineteenth centuries was not that there were too few works by Rublev, but too many. 'Old Believers' were particularly keen to acquire icons that dated from before the Schism of the 1660s (after which icons might be tainted by new doctrines), and every collector of antiquities would need a painting 'from Rublev's hand' in his collection; the result naturally was that no serious person believed in any of them.

They were not yet, of course, assessed as works of art, let alone masterpieces. Rublev makes no appearance in Russia's first major encyclopedia (Brockhaus and Efron, 1890–1907). Yet when, soon after the Revolution, Lenin devised a 'Scheme of Monumental Propaganda' (overseen by Vladimir Tatlin), intended to remove 'monuments erected in honour of Tsars and their servants, and the production of monuments to the Russian socialist revolution', there, astonishingly, was Rublev's name among the first list of 66 figures suggested for such commemoration.[25]

A shift of mood can be felt with the arrival of scholars into the field, and to look at some of them may be instructive. The first of these, who entered the art-historical realm in the 1860s and towered over it for many decades, was Nikodim Kondakov (1844–1925). Though he claimed he found both aesthetic enjoyment and spiritual satisfaction in Byzantine and Old Russian art, he has been termed an archaeologist of the icon, an immensely conscientious assembler of precise factual detail. He also knew Italian *trecento* art – itself becoming of interest as more than merely 'primitive' – and was in no doubt as to where Old Russian art derived from: the 'Italo-Cretan' school, largely on the basis of insecurely dated pictures of the Mother of God. He was unlucky in being too old to take on board the great Rublev discoveries, having emigrated in 1920 (he set up a foundation to carry on his work in Prague).[26]

The difference a generation can make is emphasized when one juxtaposes Kondakov with Pavel Muratov (1881–1950). He too had expert knowledge of early Italian art, as well as the Old Russian monuments, and he too lived outside Russia after 1922. But Muratov was also well acquainted with the recent Viennese formalistic approach embodied in Wölfflin, Riegl and others, allowing him to appreciate the specific cultural language of the icon on its own terms, while keeping up to date with advances in the general and art history of Byzantium. The whole 'Italo-Cretan' idea was revealed as a red herring, as too were persistent attempts to derive everything from Sienese or other *trecento* Italian masters. Instead he put the study of Old Russian art on a methodologically secure basis, deriving as it did from the Byzantine, with a folk-based admixture. The age of Rublev was clearly in direct descent from the 'Palaeologan Renaissance', the last period (post-1261) of Byzantine artistic development, with its notably revived Hellenistic impulse.

Two more scholarly specialists in the icon take things further than Muratov, into realms of deep subjectivity: Nikolay Punin (1888–1953) and Pavel Florensky (1882–1937). Each had a special link with Rublev; neither emigrated, becoming prominent figures in the Soviet Union, though both were eventually imprisoned (and Florensky executed). Punin was an astonishingly productive writer, and on starting work at the St Petersburg Russian Museum (with its large collection of icons) in 1913 – the same year as a major exhibition in Moscow of Old Russian art, celebrating the tercentenary of the Romanov dynasty – produced a stream of articles, some of which became independent publications. These included the first booklet on Rublev's manner of painting, written incredibly before the first adequate display of the *Old Testament Trinity* (1915). In a letter he wrote that 'the whole of European art (perhaps only with the exception of the Renaissance) – looks like toys.'[27] The remarkable dimension to all this is that Punin became known as a major proponent of modernism. While he was immersed in ancient icons, he was simultaneously praising Vladimir Tatlin as the hero of the new art. He was the first serious critic to tie Old Russian art to the Modern movement – something that came naturally to Russia, but would have been strange in Italy or other Western European countries (illus. 57).

Florensky's life is scarcely believable, and not easy to summarize. Born in the Caucasus, son of a Russian railway engineer and Armenian mother, he was a highly promising mathematician with a strong all-round interest in the natural sciences – but rejected the offer of postgraduate work at Moscow University, convinced that Cantor's set theory and other manifestations of indeterminacy demonstrated the existence of God. He decided to train for the priesthood, and set up house with his new family in 1911 at Sergiev Posad, beside St Sergius's Trinity Monastery. At the same time he grew close to the modern Symbolist poets and thinkers. He wrote and published copiously on theological and philosophical matters, yet his natural-scientific and mathematical interests did not leave him, and if anything broadened. After the Revolution this stood him in good stead, though somewhat provocatively he wore priestly garments even at Soviet committee meetings. Even in exile, after arrest on a completely spurious charge in 1933 (rescinded in 1958), he continued to work unstoppably.

From our point of view, however, the central moment of his life came when, shortly after the Revolution, he became a leading member of the committee charged with cataloguing the vast

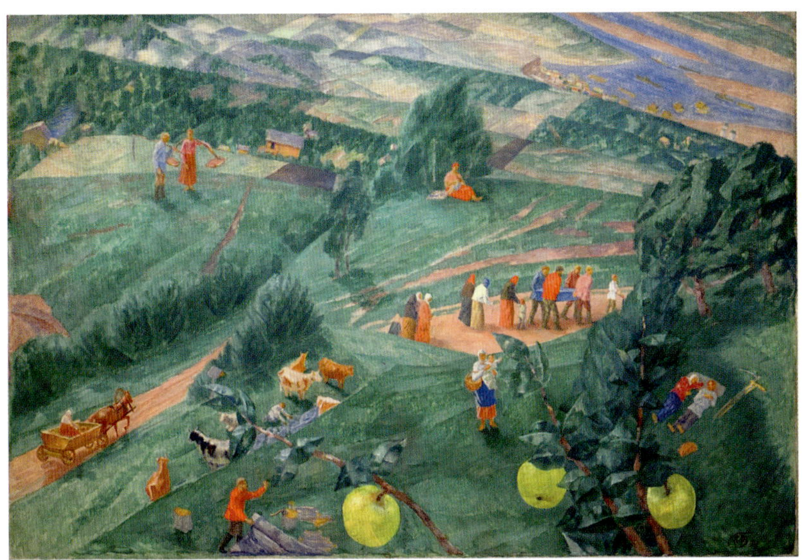

57 Kuzma Petrov-Vodkin, *Midday, Summer*, 1917, oil on canvas. From a
poor family on the middle Volga, Petrov-Vodkin, a symbolist rather than
extreme modernist artist – familiar all his life with icons – developed
his own curvilinear perspective, having much in common with iconic
picture-space and often employing semi-transparent planes (as did
Tatlin) and pure iconic colours. This painting encapsulates the
middle-Volga landscape and derives too from his father's funeral.

number of treasures at the monastery. This led to the serious
investigations of the iconostasis and reverse perspective on
which his fame largely rests today. He pungently dismissed post-
Renaissance perspective as a 'stage show', and argued that the
truest cognition of reality could be attained by creatively ignor-
ing it. Less well known is his remarkable sensitivity to colour –
notably the shades of azure that are a favoured resource of Rublev.
With several other figures of distinction, notably his artist sister
Raisa and Russia's greatest printmaker, Vladimir Favorsky, who
lived nearby until the end of the 1930s (and survived to design
the invitation to the first post-war Rublev conference), he set
up the inspirational modernist group 'Makovets' – for him, the
hill mentioned in Chapter Four, on which Sergius's monastery

is set, was the centrepiece of Russian culture: its 'living node' or 'source'. He pushed unsuccessfully for the monastic way of life to be preserved as a living museum. He was one of the first people to witness the restoration of the *Old Testament Trinity* in 1919; within the year this moved him to an ecstatic commentary that puts more sober Soviet art history in the shade:

> In Rublev's work what moves, astonishes and all but sets us alight is in no way the subject-matter, nor the number 'three', nor the chalice on the table, but the suddenly torn-down veil of the noumenal world in front of us . . . he having truly presented us with a discovery that he himself perceived . . . an azure loftier than anything in existence.[28]

Famously he claimed, 'There exists Rublev's icon of the Trinity, therefore God exists.' With possibly inappropriate levity, he told his first interrogators that he was a 'specialist in electrical engineering', but in politics 'a medieval, approximately 14th century, Romantic'.[29] He and many others were taken away in a dreadful last spasm of the Yezhov terror – the worst period of the purges of the late 1930s. A few months later, when Yezhov was deposed and arrested, things could have worked out differently.

From the end of the 1920s Soviet official policy towards relics of Orthodox culture – including icons – hardened. In true 'vulgar sociological' spirit they were taken as expressing the oppressive values of the ruling class, yet mostly remained in museums, with suitably adjusted labels. It was hard to keep interest in Rublev scholarship alive, but it happened: the figure most responsible was the elusive Igor Grabar (1871–1960). Long before the Revolution he had not only made a considerable name for himself as a Symbolist painter but had started editing, and partly writing, the first great multi-volume history of Russian art. Thereafter he led expeditions to discover, and (perhaps too speedily) restore lost masterpieces: without him, the Zvenigorod icons would have been mere firewood. Unsuccessful in several campaigns to preserve historic buildings, he retreated back to his own painting in the mid-1930s, but re-emerged as an advisor: Stalin seems to have trusted his judgement. Nevertheless a new generation of art historians was emerging from under Grabar's wing, and cautiously took up Byzantine and Old Russian themes, grasping the opportunity offered by Stalin's wartime deal with the Orthodox Church – which incidentally occasioned the reopening of the Trinity Monastery.

Of these, Viktor Lazarev (1897–1976) was first to make his name: his massive and up-to-date *History of Byzantine Art* appeared in 1948. A major and authoritative scholar, he later turned to books on Rublev and Feofan. Only slightly younger was Mikhail Alpatov (1902–1986), a scholar of great sensitivity whose short, poorly illustrated book on Rublev, as early as 1943, was the first monograph on the artist. The (mostly) polite rivalry between the two of them became legendary. Lazarev was dogmatic, well informed and knew just what he thought of late Byzantium – that in the mid-fourteenth century its intellectual life was captured by backward-looking clerics allied with the Hesychast spiritual movement, and things went downhill from the classicizing glories of the Constantinople Church of the Chora (*c.* 1320) thereafter. Taking up Wölfflin's distinction between 'linear' and 'painterly' art, he made a good case for the linearity of not only the despised Italo-Cretan products – a dead end in art – but late Byzantine painting in general. He saw Feofan as escaping from this atmosphere.

As for Rublev, it is unclear where this scheme leaves him: obviously a painterly master (though with linear strengths), he can hardly have escaped the Hesychasm that pervades Yepifany's life of St Sergius – it had anyhow been official Orthodox doctrine since 1351. Alpatov's well-produced volume of 1972 is far more nuanced. To single out just these two is hard, in all fairness, on the many younger art historians who have made exact and exacting (if occasionally weird) contributions to Rublevology since.

It was not, however, an art expert but the great cultural historian Dmitriy Likhachov (1906–1999) who, with his unrivalled knowledge of Russian and Slavic medieval chronicles and saints' lives, wove the whole culture of the age together in what he termed the 'Orthodox pre-Renaissance', with his concise if awkwardly titled study *Russian Culture in the Age of Andrey Rublev and Yepifaniy the Wise* (1962). Its scope of attention to the entire 'Byzantine Commonwealth' makes it impossible for any subsequent scholar to ignore. So, differently, is the first and only biography of Rublev to have been published, in the famous Russian series (dating from the nineteenth century) *Lives of Notable People*, by Valeriy Sergeyev (1982; translated into various languages, but not English). It is a strange, densely written book, over two hundred pages long, speculating from an imaginative recreation of the historical background in an attempt to fill the all-too-many gaps in Rublev's life. The author worked for years at the ancient Andronikov Monastery, in which, surprisingly but gratifyingly, Stalin set up the Andrey Rublev Museum in the late 1940s – Sergeyev's preface gives us some information on this. As far as art-historical matters are concerned, Sergeyev tends simply to quote the main specialists.

The book nonetheless is a sort of classic. As for exhibitions, the 650th anniversary display at the Tretyakov Gallery, Moscow, of 2010 was in a class of its own, showing *inter alia* many fragments of painted plaster from beneath floor level in buildings where Rublev worked, with an immense catalogue imbued with up-to-date knowledge and compiled by the best scholars now working in the field. By that time, before the end of the USSR,

Andrey Rublev had already been canonized (1988), with his feast day decreed on 4 July (os), the day of the early Christian hymnographer and notable defender of icons St Andrew of Crete – not, as might have been expected, the apostle Andrew.

Nothing could compare, however, in producing an image of Rublev for the modern age, with Tarkovsky's film of 1966. It was really his first independent work – *Ivan's Childhood*, memorable as it is, took up someone else's script – and is in its way the jumping-off point for the rest of his career. Tarkovsky was certainly giving hostages to fortune. The whole thing, even when somewhat shortened, lasts over 180 minutes, and is deliberately episodic, though making a point of using incredibly long takes – a rebuttal of Eisenstein's montage ('sculpting in time' was the

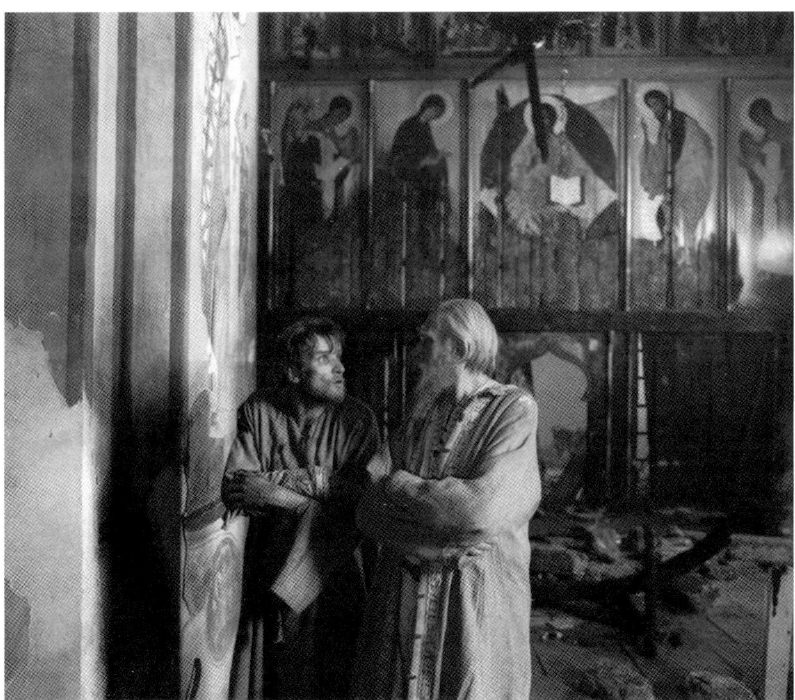

58 Scene where Rublev (left) meets Feofan Grek in semi-decorated church, from Tarkovsky's film *Andrei Rublev* (1966).

term Tarkovsky himself used for his method). These episodes
are given precise dates, implying a degree of historical exacti-
tude that Tarkovsky never really claimed; authentic persons and
events are mixed with fictional ones. What interests Tarkovsky
is the true artist's 'leap of faith' into the unknown and the numi-
nous – whether in trying to fly from a church roof (first episode)
or casting a great bell without the knowhow (final episode – a
film in itself). But he certainly did his homework: still in his
twenties, Tarkovsky and his co-writer, Konchalovsky (another
Andrey, at the time of writing still working), spent the two
years after the film was approved (1963) reading up on Russian
medieval history, art and literature. An unknown actor from
Sverdlovsk in Siberia, Anatoliy Solonitsyn, turned up and suc-
cessfully demanded to audition for the part of Rublev (illus. 58).

The Soviet authorities got more than they had bargained
for: after one showing in 1966, and one more a couple of years
later at Cannes, the cat was out of the bag, and the film's success
became unstoppable. As Tarkovsky said: 'I think what they did
not like in my work were not the ideas, but the artistic form: the
mere fact that a phenomenon called "art" may exist at all . . .
The strength of art is itself . . . which cannot be subjected either
to the will of individuals or of political systems.'[30] Tarkovsky
leads his Rublev into a spiritual crisis in which he abandons
not only painting (we never see him at work, incidentally), but
speech itself. In the end both seem to be restored, and the film,
after three hours in black-and-white, ends with a postscript in
a blaze of colour, as the camera slowly dwells on details of the
real Rublev's iconic works, and thence to a final shot of horses,
symbol of life, standing in the rain (a frequent backdrop to the
action).

Some people hated the film, and among the most outspoken
was the exiled Solzhenitsyn: he claimed not only that Tarkovsky
had misunderstood and misrepresented Christianity, but that

he had done violence to Rublev's life and times, during which in reality he moved calmly from one commission to the next. Violence was indeed an issue: some of the scenes are stomach-turning. Yet in real life there actually were savage Tatar raids; there was a Patrikey, brutally killed; there were princely feuds, as well as considerable peaceful periods. Such problems cannot be simply resolved, as Solzhenitsyn, no slouch himself at fictional re-enactments of history, must have realized. Sergeyev inclined to Solzhenitsyn's view (as did Alpatov) and reveals that Tarkovsky told him that he himself was the true subject of the film (many an auteur has said as much).[31] Robert Bird deftly characterizes the film itself as a 'celluloid icon'.[32] But its true subject is the (very difficult) restoration of harmony, after it has been in one way or another disrupted, in human existence.

SEVEN

Summing Up

Can we – indeed, should we – sum up Rublev? An icon painter from whose brush only one definite work, and that much damaged, survives? We can add three more that are unchallenged, and a few more dubiously, but only as a supposition. Luckily the astonishing wall paintings of the Vladimir cathedral are also with us, even if precariously, and they are his most extensive memorial. He certainly had vision – it seems (with Daniil) he was the inventor of that magnificent feature the high iconostasis. He was entirely a figure of the late Byzantine 'Palaiologan renaissance'[33] – there is no evidence or likelihood that Western European currents affected him – while transcending its norms at every point. To call him 'the Russian Fra Angelico', as is sometimes done, diminishes both of them – though it is possible that we recognize in him a quality which transcends normal boundaries, 'that withdrawn, dignified air' of quattrocento faces.[34] Alpatov wisely pointed out, however, that, while Western art of the *trecento* was wrapped up in allegory, Rublev's work is steeped in symbolism.[35]

Understated perfection of form, colour and tone is where his strength lies. Together they leave an unforgettable sense of big-heartedness, openness to all experience, gravity and a classically based decorum mixed with a certain playfulness; all qualities, as it happens, that attract Russians to their greatest poet, Alexander Pushkin (1799–1837). Thus Alpatov, putting aside normal scholarly restraint, was able to write:

> In the history of the arts there is no other one work
> that, to the same extent as the *Trinity*, embodies the
> best spiritual forces of an entire nation. If Rublev's *Trinity*
> were the only old Russian painting to come down to us,
> a thoughtful historian should be able to discern from it
> the whole culture of the people who created it – the
> character of this people, its ideals and aspirations.[36]

Lest this be thought of as just an example of Soviet grandiloquence, the Oxford scholar Dimitri Obolensky unequivocally called Rublev 'the greatest Russian artist who ever lived', revealing within 'a pure Constinopolitan manner . . . a clarity of composition and a suave tranquillity of mood peculiarly his own'.[37]

Rublev attained high status in his own time, casting his spell on art for the rest of his century, yet was then forgotten, save as an occasional name to conjure with. Quite strangely, he has become a central figure of Russian culture, leaping to that position little over a hundred years ago, since when he has been declared an Orthodox saint. Meanwhile his own contribution to the 'Sergievan' age was not just one of promise but achievement, as his life's work (to the extent we can judge it) shows. To have two painters of such genius as Rublev and Feofan working in Russia at the same time was an extraordinary blessing.

In fact – risky as it is to generalize about whole periods in such a way – in Russia the time of Rublev, around 1400, was rather a good one, despite the Tatars and the Black Death. Prosperity and trade were expanding, as was settlement of the forest zone. Building work took off. Princes were beginning to manage their arguments without resorting to hostilities. As Byzantium struggled, Russia (assisted by the Balkan Slavs) was on the up. It had avoided, more or less, the turmoil that the fourteenth century had brought to much of Europe: the 'Peasants' Revolt' and its bloody consequences, heresies and witchcraft trials, the Papal schism, the Hundred Years War – such things were to change in the next century.

On the last page of Otto Demus's magisterial work *Byzantine Art and the West* (1970), the Viennese art historian sums up what his book is about:

> [Byzantium] helped to make Western art an instrument for shaping and propagating ideas in monumental form and helped it, as well, to instil into human figures and their actions a kind of dignity and a feeling of life; it transmitted and revived age-old standards of harmony in form and colour; and it gave the medieval West a first taste of humanism – not the superficial humanism of the intellect, but a deeper humanism of the spirit. And, finally, it transmitted an expert knowledge of the painterly use of colour and its effects. This was possible only because Byzantine art was the living continuation of Greek art and so was able to lead Western artists back to the classical sources.

Readers who have got this far will realize every one of these phrases can without strain be applied to Rublev and his age. However Rublev came by his feeling for classicism (we have mentioned some possibilities), it is unmistakable in what we know of him from first to last. You need only to have studied the Romanesque and early Gothic wall paintings of the West to know that he is in a different, and highly sophisticated, league.

Yet he is not a Byzantine manqué, and is never tied down to Hellenistic models. This can easily be seen if we compare a fine

Byzantine icon of the Twelve Apostles (*c.* 1300), in the Pushkin Art Museum, Moscow, used by Demus on his dust jacket, with a similar scene in the Vladimir wall paintings. Splendid as the colour effects in the Byzantine icon are, the figures themselves are curiously stiff and uninteresting – an amateur dramatic society got up in togas – compared with the ease and grace of the Vladimir figures.

But perhaps we should continue to the last sentences of Demus's work:

> Byzantium was able to play a part in this process only because of the ability of Western artists to see the Greek behind the Byzantine. How all-important this was can, perhaps, be realized if, for a moment, we try to imagine artists who were as deeply influenced by Byzantine art but had no possibility of referring back to the classical sources of Byzantium. Such artists did, in fact, exist: namely, the icon painters of Russia. They too were disciples of Byzantium, but they never became students of antiquity. Thus, their way did not lead to a renaissance or a new humanism. It lost itself in the decorative mazes of folk art.[38]

Those folksy mazes did indeed become apparent (though whether icon painting 'lost itself' in them is more than questionable), but not for a good 150 years after Rublev's time.

Not all works attributed to Rublev would normally be called icons, but he is so firmly anchored in what one would broadly term the 'iconic world' that a note to introduce the latter to a readership perhaps unfamiliar with it may not be out of place here. Equally, the history of the period merits a brief subsequent chronology of events relevant to the text.

An 'icon' is an image (it is a Greek word, taken over into Russian and other Slavonic languages as *ikona*). Early in the Christian period it came to imply the image of a sacred person or event used as a focus for prayer. Legend has it that Christ himself miraculously produced the first such icon, the self-image 'Not Made by Hands', on a cloth sent to heal King Abgar of Edessa; St Luke, depicting the Mother of God, was supposedly the first icon painter.

Traditionally in Russia a novice icon painter's first task would be a replica of the icon 'Not Made by Hands'. Icons were thought of as accurate, realistic representations of holy personages and events from biblical times and subsequently; medieval people, visited by saints in their dreams, would recognize them from their iconic images. Icons, though, are not simply illustrative or didactic, as much Western religious art has been. It would be beyond the scope of this book to investigate their sacred meaning within Orthodox theology, on which much has been written, but the basic message is generally clear – as Christ and the saints took on material form to convey their message, so the icon with its material image realizes it for the worshipper.

Icons almost occasioned a civil war in the East Roman (Byzantine) Empire when in the early eighth century the Church and state authorities – following the Second Commandment against 'graven images' and 'likenesses' (Exodus 20:4) – banned them, so instigating the long period of iconoclasm. This was resisted by the poor and unprivileged, by monks, by women, by provincials, and ultimately (in 843) the iconoclast elite capitulated. Images were restored, in what was celebrated as the 'Feast of Orthodoxy'. Since then, it has been made clear that icons have been (in theory, at least) not superstitiously worshipped, but venerated as a two-way channel of communication with the higher world. For the Orthodox believer, seeing was believing: every saint had to have an iconic image. Icons – accessible to all classes of a largely illiterate society – were a great force for social cohesion in the Orthodox lands, which stretched from Venice through Siberia to Alaska, and from the Nile to beyond the Arctic Circle.

The term 'icon' can have a broad sense, including devotional objects of many kinds, wall paintings, mosaics, textiles, images of carved wood or metal, whole buildings, monasteries, cities (above all Constantinople and Jerusalem, eventually to be joined by Moscow), certain written texts and musical compositions, even holy persons. More commonly and more narrowly, though, it applies to paintings for veneration (as we have seen) on portable wooden panels. This is not surprising: by the nineteenth century millions upon millions of them were produced, above all in Russia (for centuries the one free Orthodox country, whose people perceived it as sanctified and protected by the heavenly grace that flowed through its countless churches, shrines and icons). The icon-screen (iconostasis), with its royal doors leading through to the sanctuary, became the focal point of church architecture. Icons could depict other icons and the miracles they wrought; icons of icons of icons are not unknown. Icons were on occasion very mobile, often carried in processions: to quote Anastasia Dandraki, 'In public life devotional icons were public figures. The devotional practices organized around them defined and were in turn defined by the cycle of life.'[39]

Panel icons consist of one or more boards (in Russia, usually lime wood; in Byzantium, cypress), secured at the back by wooden struts, often with the facial side somewhat hollowed; with time, and the effect of water vapour on the unpainted side, the panel would usually become 'bowed', that is, convex, though this was not intended. Painting would be done in egg tempera on a carefully prepared fine plaster base; an oil-based varnish (which would usually darken after a few decades) would then be applied. Old icons would seldom be discarded, but were either scraped down for reuse or overpainted.

From the painter's point of view he was 'revealing' an already extant image rather than deliberately exercising his own creativity. He was performing a traditional task in an established way, and images were not subject to alteration at whim. (As G. H. Hamilton puts it, 'An icon was neither a literal representation nor an abstract symbol.'[40] Nevertheless stylistic changes did happen over the course of time, and many variant local manners and types of icon evolved, particularly in Russia. All are ultimately rooted in Byzantine artistic practice, itself a development of the classical art of late antiquity. However stiff, stylized or anti-naturalistic icons may sometimes look to us, their clear, harmonious colours, ordering of gesture, folds of drapery and so on speak of a classic heritage.

One often-noticed aspect of their pictorial language is the so-called reverse perspective often apparent in the setting of iconic figures: unlike in post-Renaissance 'true' perspective, there seems to be a vanishing point projected forwards from the surface, drawing the spectator into a transcendental realm. But there was another iconic pictorial language, that of colour: heavenly gold, holy blue and deep red, worldly greens and browns.

Icons may be gateways into another world, but they are also emphatically physical objects: their materials – wood, sometimes elaborate metal casings, even jewels – are obvious and unconcealed. Domestic icons, respected as they would be, were objects of household utility, almost members of the household (thanked when things went well, on occasion blamed if they went badly): guests would greet them and be seated near them. Villagers and townsfolk would have icons in church that they held in special reverence and affection; a few might be wonder-working, a channel for miracles. They were an essential, rather than optional or decorative, part of Orthodox culture: they were indeed works of art, yet more importantly belonged to a realm of experience superior to the merely artistic. By the nineteenth century the demand for icons was huge, involving factory methods and a nationwide distribution system.

This chimed with the quest of many figures in modernist art movements from the turn of the nineteenth and twentieth centuries onwards, beginning with the Symbolists, who like icon painters strove for artistic transcendence. Bored by the superficiality of nineteenth-century realism, sickened by the slickness of nineteenth-century techniques, they found in icons an art whose qualities went beyond style, individualism, representationalism or mere decoration. Simultaneously, modern restoration methods began to reveal medieval icons in their full nobility and power. Henri Matisse (in 1911) was one of the first whose enthusiasm for icons spread their repute and influence far beyond the Orthodox lands; it has continued rippling outwards ever since.

This note would be incomplete if the iconostasis went without description. In its fullest, 'high', version it dates (so far as we know) from the time of Rublev and his colleague Daniil, who may well have instigated it in the tall Dormition Cathedral at Vladimir. It is an astonishing Russian contribution not just to Orthodox devotion but to world art. It rises in tier after tier on a wooden frame towards the roof, but always its main – tallest – element is the 'Deisis' composition, centred on an awe-inspiring figure of Christ in Majesty, flanked by John the Baptist and the Mother of God, turned towards him and interceding for humanity. They in turn are flanked by saints. Above (usually) is a much smaller, and livelier, set of scenes of the major Feasts of the Church; the Kremlin Annunciation cathedral has a miniature 'Menology' row beneath the Deisis. Above them the Prophets wave their texts, and higher still there may be Patriarchs. Finally we descend to earth with the 'local tier (see illus. 20) of icons, particularly meaningful and close to the congregation, interrupted by the royal doors; how and when this tier developed is uncertain, but it has often contained some remarkable and ancient icons, notably of course the Rublev *Old Testament Trinity*.

Later – well after Rublev – we get further elaborations in the icon's history: complex calendar icons, miniature travelling iconostases, folding multi-leaved (often metal) icons and many other variants.

CHRONOLOGY

862	Legendary invitation to the Varangians (Vikings) to 'come and rule us'
988/9	Conversion of Vladimir I to Christianity
1037–c. 1047	Construction of Santa Sophia in Kiev
1054	Schism between Eastern and Western Churches formalized
1110s	Compilation of Russian Primary Chronicle
1147	First Chronicle mention of Moscow
1158	Building of Cathedral of Dormition in Vladimir begins; repaired and enlarged after 1183
1169	Andrey 'Bogolyubskiy' sacks Kiev
1185	Prince Igor's unsuccessful expedition against the Polovtsians, subject of the 'Igor Tale'
1193/4	Construction of palace church of St Dmitriy, Vladimir
1204–61	Fourth Crusade captures and occupies Constantinople
1220–24	Building of St George, Yuriev-Polskiy, last Vladimir-style church with carvings
1237–40	Tatar conquest of Rus
1240	Novgorod Prince Alexander 'Nevsky' defeats Swedes on Neva river
1242	Alexander defeats Teutonic Knights in 'Battle on the Ice' of Lake Peipus
1299	Metropolitan of Kiev and All Rus moves to Vladimir
1320s (*late*)	Metropolitan moves to Moscow
1321–1392	Lifetime of St Sergius (originally Varfolomey) of Radonezh
1326	Construction of Cathedral of Dormition, probably first stone building in Moscow
1331 (*probably*)–41	Ivan I 'Kalita' of Moscow is Grand Prince of Vladimir
1340–1396	Lifetime of St Stephen of Perm
1341–51	Councils of Constantinople (affirming Hesychasm)
1362	Prince Dmitriy Ivanovich of Moscow becomes Grand Prince of Vladimir
1365–6	First major outbreak of Black Death in Russian lands

1360s (*probably*)	Birth of Rublev
1378	First mention of Feofan (Theophanes the Greek), in Novgorod. Battle of the Vozha (near Ryazan) – defeat of Tatar force
1380	Dmitriy defeats Tatar army of Mamai at Kulikovo; thereafter is known as 'Donskoy'
1389	Death of Dmitriy, leaving appanage of Zvenigorod to son Yuriy
1395	Feofan and team paint Archangel Michael Cathedral in Moscow Kremlin
1397	Foundation of Kirillov Monastery
c. 1399	Dormition Cathedral of Zvenigorod built
c. 1400	Zvenigorod range of icons painted
1405	Annunciation Cathedral in Kremlin painted by Feofan, Prokhor and Andrey
1407	Metropolitan Kiprian (instigator of Trinity Chronicle) dies
1408	'Great stone church' in Vladimir (re)painted by Daniil and Andrey. (December) Tatar leader Edigey devastates central Russia
1425–50	Dynastic struggle for throne of Moscow
c. 1425	Daniil and Andrey paint new stone Cathedral of Trinity Monastery
1420s (*late*)	Andrey paints new Cathedral of Andronikov Monastery
1430	(29 January) Andrey dies (according to lost gravestone), followed by Daniil
1439–1515	Lifetime of St Joseph of Volokolamsk
1453	Fall of Constantinople to Ottoman Turks
1462	Ivan III (the 'Great') comes to throne of Moscow
1478	Novgorod incorporated into Moscow
1480	Moscow ceases to pay tribute to the Tatars
1502	Dionisiy and sons paint Ferapontov Monastery Cathedral
1551	Stoglav ('Council of 100 Chapters'), commends Rublev's *Old Testament Trinity* as exemplary
1773/4	High iconostasis of Vladimir Dormition Cathedral dismantled and sold
1904, 1919	*Old Testament Trinity* icon cleaned
1947	Andrey Rublev Museum established in former Andronikov Monastery

1988 Canonization of Andrey Rublev and Dmitriy Donskoy as Orthodox saints

REFERENCES

1 Donald Allchin, 'Icons and Their Meaning for Today', in *Icons 88*, ed. S. Smyth and S. Kingston (Dublin, 1988), p. 129.

2 Amy Gillette, 'The Music of Angels in Byzantine and Post-Byzantine Art', *Peregrinations*, VI/4 (2018), pp. 26–78 (pp. 27–8).

3 Quoted and discussed in John Milner, *Kazimir Malevich and the Art of Geometry* (London, 1996), p. 81.

4 Stella Rock, *Popular Religion in Russia: 'Double Belief' and the Making of an Academic Myth* (Abingdon, 2007), p. 17 et seq.

5 Robin Milner-Gulland, 'Russia's Lost Renaissance', in *Literature and Western Civilization*, vol. IV, ed. A. Thorlby and D. Daiches (London, 1974), pp. 435–68.

6 Roman Jakobson and Dean Worth, *Sofonija's Tale of the Russian-Tatar Battle on the Kulikovo Field* (The Hague, 1963).

7 Janet Martin, *Medieval Russia, 980–1584* (Cambridge, 1995), p. 222.

8 Robin Milner-Gulland and Antony Bryer, 'Two Metropolitans of Trebizond in Russia', in *Archeion Pontou*, vol. XXVII (Athens, 1965), pp. 21–7.

9 Dmitriy Likhachov, *Izbranniye trudy po russkoy i mirovoy kulture* (St Petersburg, 2006), pp. 87–163.

10 Valeriy Sergeyev, *Andrey Rublev* (Moscow, 1982), pp. 61–2.

11 Tatyana Vilinbakhova in *Gates of Mystery: The Art of Holy Russia*, exh. cat., Dallas Museum of Art (Fort Worth, TX, 1993), p. 232.

12 I. Kachalova et al., *Blagoveshensky sobor Moskovskogo kremlya* (Moscow, 1990), ch. 2.

13 Mikhail Alpatov, *Andrey Rublev* (Moscow 1972), p. 39.

14 Gerold Vzdornov, 'Medieval Russian Manuscripts', in *The Art of Holy Russia: Icons from Moscow, 1400–1600*, ed. Robin Cormack and Delia Gaze, exh. cat., Royal Academy of Art, London (1997), p. 64.

15 Robin Milner-Gulland, *Patterns of Russia* (London, 2020), pp. 97–8.

16 Viktor Lazarev, *Feofan Grek* (Moscow, 1961), pp. 8–10, 113–14 (my translation). Edigey (or Edigu), Emir of the White (or Nogay) Horde, raided Russia in 1408 and destroyed the wooden

Trinity Monastery. Yepifaniy's request is of antiquarian interest, since it refers to the tall statue of Justinian (holding an 'apple'), subsequently destroyed by the Ottomans.

17 Robin Cormack, *Byzantine Art* (Oxford, 2000), p. 213.

18 See Anita Strezova, *Hesychasm and Art* (Canberra, 2014).

19 V. Baranov in *Savvinskiye chteniya*, 4 (2019), pp. 198–200.

20 George Hamilton, *The Art and Architecture of Russia* [1954] (London, 1983), p. 139.

21 Viktor Lazarev, *Old Russian Murals and Mosaics* (London, 1966).

22 Agnes Kriza, 'Legitimizing the Rublev Trinity', *Byzantinoslavica*, 74 (2016), pp. 134–52.

23 Dmitry Shvidkovsky, *Russian Architecture and the West* (New Haven, CT, 2007), p. 70.

24 Ibid., p. 66.

25 Christina Lodder, *Russian Constructivism* (London, 1983), p. 53.

26 Kondakovian attitudes lingered on, particularly in the West – the notable, if eccentric, scholar Fr Gervase Mathew wrote: 'A close study of the Old Testament Trinity attributed to Andrei Rublev has led me to conclude that it is most probably Constantinopolitan of *c*. 1400. This would explain the obvious relationship with Sienese *trecento* painting – so inexplicable in early 15th century Moscow': Mathew, *Byzantine Aesthetics* (London, 1963), p. 168, n. 2. It is reasonable to guess that Rublev's use of ultramarine led him to this association with Siena.

27 Natalia Murray, 'The Role of the "Red Commissar" Nikolay Punin in the Rediscovery of Icons', in *Modernism and the Spiritual in Russian Art*, ed. Louise Hardiman and Nicola Kozicharow (London, 2017), p. 218.

28 In Gerold Vzdornov, ed., *Troitsa Andreya Rubleva – Antologiya* (Moscow, 1989), pp. 52–3.

29 Avril Pyman, *Pavel Florensky: A Quiet Genius* (London, 2010), p. 156.

30 Anna Lawton, 'Art and Religion in the Films of Andrei Tarkovskii', in *Christianity and the Arts in Russia*, ed. William Craft Brumfield and Milos Velimirovic (Cambridge, 1991), p. 152.

31 Sergeyev, *Andrey Rublev*, pp. 22–4.

32 Robert Bird, 'Tarkovsky and the Celluloid Icon', in *Alter Icons: The Russian Icon and Modernity*, ed. Jefferson J. A. Gatrall and Douglas Greenfield (Philadelphia, PA, 2010), ch. 11.

33 Alpatov, *Andrey Rublev*, p. 134.

34 John Bayley, *Iris* (London, 1998), p. 126.

35 Probably the best location in which to compare Rublev's art (particularly the Vladimir frescoes) with that of the Palaeologan Renaissance is the deserted city of Mistras, Greece, which has several well-preserved sets of fourteenth- and fifteenth-century wall paintings.
36 Mikhail Alpatov, *Art Treasures of Russia* (London, 1968), p. 132.
37 Dimitri Obolensky, *The Byzantine Commonwealth* (London, 1971), pp. 360–61.
38 Otto Demus, *Byzantine Art and the West* (London, 1970), pp. 39–40.
39 A. Dandraki et al., eds, *Heaven and Earth: Art of Byzantium from the Greek Collections*, exh. cat., National Gallery of Art, Washington, and the J. P. Getty Museum, Los Angeles (Athens, 2013), p. 111.
40 George Hamilton, *The Art and Architecture of Russia* [1954] (London, 1983), p. 99.

SELECT BIBLIOGRAPHY

Alpatov, Mikhail, *Andrey Rublev* (Moscow, 1972)
—, *Art Treasures of Russia* (London, 1968)
Bocharov, Genrikh, and Vsevolod Vygolov, *Vologda, Kirillov, Ferapontovo, Belozersk* (Moscow, 1968)
Bogdanovic, J., 'The Moveable Canopy: The Performative Space of the Major Sakkos of Metropolitan Photios', *Byzantinoslavica*, LXXII/1–2 (2014), pp. 247–92
Brumfield, William, and Milos Velimirovic, *Christianity and the Arts in Russia* (Cambridge, 1991)
Bryusova, V., *Andrey Rublev* (Moscow, 1995)
Bunge, Gabriel, *The Rublev Trinity*, trans. Andrew Louth (New York, 2005)
Cormack, Robin, *Byzantine Art* (Oxford, 2000)
Demus, Otto, *Byzantine Art and the West* (London, 1970)
Dandraki, A., 'Icons in the Devotional Practices of Byzantium', in *Heaven and Earth: Art of Byzantium from the Greek Collections*, ed. Drandaki et al., exh. cat., National Gallery of Art, Washington, and the J. P. Getty (Athens, 2013), pp. 109–14
Faensen, Hubert, and Vladimir Ivanov, *Early Russian Architecture* (London, 1975)
Florensky, Pavel, *Beyond Vision*, ed. Nicoletta Misler, trans. Wendy Salmond (London, 2002)
Franklin, Simon, and Jonathan Shepard, *The Emergence of Rus, 750–1200* (London, 1996)
Frankopan, Peter, *The Silk Roads* (London, 2015)
Gatrall, Jefferson J. A., and Douglas Greenfield, *Alter Icons: The Russian Icon and Modernity* (Philadelphia, PA, 2010)
Gillette, Amy, 'The Music of Angels in Byzantine and Post-Byzantine Art', *Peregrinations*, VI/4 (2018), pp. 26–78
Goleyzovsky, N., and S. Yamshchikov, *Feofan Grek i yego shkola* (Moscow, 1970)
Guseva, E., A. *Rublev iz sobraniya Tretyakovskoy Gallereyi* (Moscow, 1990)
Hamilton, George, *The Art and Architecture of Russia* [1954] (London, 1983)

Hardiman, Louise, and Nicola Kozicharow, *Modernism and the Spiritual in Russian Art* (London, 2017)

Jakobson, Roman, and Dean Worth, *Sofonija's Tale of the Russian-Tatar Battle on the Kulikovo Field* (The Hague, 1963)

Kaiser, Daniel, and Gary Marker, eds, *Reinterpreting Russian History* (Oxford, 1994)

Karger, M., *Drevnerusskaya monumentalnaya zhivopis* (Moscow/ Leningrad, 1963)

Kriza, Agnes, 'Legitimizing the Rublev Trinity', *Byzantinoslavica*, 74 (2016), pp. 134–52

Lazarev, Viktor, *Andrey Rublev* (Moscow, 1970)

—, *Feofan Grek i yego shkola* (Moscow, 1961)

—, *Istoriya Vizantiyskoy zhivopisi* (Moscow, 1947)

—, *Old Russian Murals and Mosaics* (London, 1966)

Lidov, Aleksey, ed., *Ogon i svet v sakralnom prostranstve* (Moscow, 2011)

Likhachov, Dmitriy, *Izbranniye trudy po russkoy i mirovoy kulturoy* (St Petersburg, 2006)

Litvin, A., ed., *Russkaya istoricheskaya mozaika* (Kazan, 2003)

Marki, E., 'Eternity', in *Heaven and Earth: Art of Byzantium from the Greek Collections*, ed. A. Drandaki et al., exh. cat., National Gallery of Art, Washington, and the J. P. Getty Museum, Los Angeles (Athens, 2013), pp. 48–50

Martin, Janet, *Medieval Russia, 980–1584* (Cambridge, 1995)

Milner, John, *Kazimir Malevich and the Art of Geometry* (London, 1996)

Milner-Gulland, Robin, *Patterns of Russia* (London, 2020)

—, 'Russia's Lost Renaissance', in *Literature and Western Civilization*, vol. IV, ed. A. Thorlby and D. Daiches (London, 1974)

Obolensky, Dimitri, *The Byzantine Commonwealth* (London, 1974)

Plugin, Vladimir, *Andrey Rublev i dukhovnaya zhizn Rusi kontsa XIV – pervoy treti XV vekov – Avtoreferat dissertatsii* (Moscow, 1994)

Pyman, Avril, *Pavel Florensky: A Quiet Genius* (London, 2010)

Rock, Stella, *Popular Religion in Russia* (Abingdon, 2007)

Ryan, William, *The Bathhouse at Midnight* (Stroud, 1999)

Sergeyev, Valeriy, *Andrey Rublev* [1982] (Moscow, 2014)

Shvidkovsky, Dmitriy, *Russian Architecture and the West* (London, 2007)

Strezova, Anita, *Hesychasm and Art* (Canberra, 2014)

Tarasov, Oleg, *Icon and Devotion*, trans. and ed. R. Milner-Gulland (London, 2002)

—, *Modern i drevniye ikony* (Moscow, 2016)

Thompson, Daniel, *The Materials and Techniques of Medieval Painting* [1936] (New York, 1956)

Smyth, Sarah, and Stanford Kingston, eds, *Icons 88* (Dublin, 1988)

Vzdornov, Gerold, *Restavratsiya i Nauka* (Moscow, 2006)

—, ed., *Troitsa Andreya Rubleva – Antologiya* (Moscow, 1989)

Worobec, Christine, 'Celebration of the Summer Solstice among
the East Slavic Peasants', in *Russkaya istoricheskaya mozaika*,
ed. A. Litvin (Kazan, 2003), pp. 91–103

Zubov, V., *Yepifaniy Premudriy i Pakhomiy Serb* (TODRL ix) (Leningrad,
1953)

Exhibition Catalogues

Cormack, Robin, and Delia Gaze, eds, *The Art of Holy Russia: Icons
from Moscow, 1400–1600*, exh. cat., Royal Academy of Art, London
(1997)

Dandraki, A., et al., eds, *Heaven and Earth: Art of Byzantium from the
Greek Collections*, exh. cat., National Gallery of Art, Washington,
and the J. P. Getty Museum, Los Angeles (Athens, 2013)

Gates of Mystery: The Art of Holy Russia, exh. cat., Dallas Museum of
Art (Fort Worth, TX, 1993)

Popov, G. V., ed., *Andrey Rublev: Podvig ikonopisaniya*, exh. cat.,
Tretyakov Gallery, Moscow (2010)

Rodionov, V. A., ed., *Dionisiy: Zhivopisets preslovushchiy*, exh. cat.,
Tretyakov Gallery, Moscow (2002)

ACKNOWLEDGEMENTS

This book, though suggested to me by the publisher as one in a series of biographies of medieval people, goes back in effect to ancient days, so far as its origin is concerned. As a postgraduate student I studied the topic 'Culture of Russia and the South Slavs in the Late Middle Ages' under the guidance of Professor Dimitri Obolensky at Oxford, and Professor Nikolay Gudziy during a year at Moscow University. I wanted (perhaps underestimating its difficulties) a subject that would span both literature and art. On returning from Moscow I was rather suddenly offered a post starting the Russian course at the new University of Sussex, where I taught for the next forty years.

Obolensky pragmatically said 'Turn what you've done into a couple of articles,' which I did; but the subject wouldn't leave me, and I revisited it from time to time over the years, in the process meeting most of the distinguished modern figures here quoted: Mikhail Alpatov, Viktor Lazarev (at 6 a.m. in Bucharest's main railway station), Roman Jakobson, Gerold Vzdornov, Vladimir Plugin, Dmitriy Likhachov (several times). The voluminous handwritten notes kept from those far-off times have been very helpful for me to revisit.

Most of the present text was written during lockdown, without access to libraries: difficult yet in some ways advantageous circumstances. This is reflected in my Select Bibliography. But nothing would have been possible without my having a copy of the massive catalogue of the 2010 Rublev exhibition in Moscow, and for sending it to me I am hugely grateful to Oleg and Alyona Tarasov, as indeed I also am to several colleagues and family members for comments on growing versions of the text, or responses to queries. But it will no doubt be obvious that this book is not all words – there are copious illustrations, beyond what might be normal in a biography, since the magnificent art of Rublev and his time is doubtless largely unfamiliar to readers, however well versed in art history they may be. For help with discussing and assembling the illustrations I am particularly grateful to Alex Ciobanu at Reaktion Books, as well as to Matt Platts and Stuart Robinson for coping with problematic scanning.

PHOTO ACKNOWLEDGEMENTS

The author and publishers wish to express their thanks to the below sources of illustrative material and/or permission to reproduce it. Some locations of artworks are also given below, in the interest of brevity:

AdobeStock: 8 (irinabal18), 12 (koromelena), 13 (VitalyTitov), 17 (slava), 22 (skostin1951), 44 and 45 (dimamoroz), 53 (borisb17), 56 (irina2005); Andronikov Monastery, Moscow: 23; Cathedral of the Archangel, Moscow: 7; Church of the Dormition at Volotovo, Novgorod: 36; Church of the Transfiguration of the Saviour on Ilyin Street, Veliky Novgorod: 33, 52; Dormition Cathedral, Moscow: 38; Dormition Cathedral, Vladimir: 39, 40, 41, 42, 43, 47, 48, 49; Dormition Cathedral, Zvenigorod: 32; JIPEN/ Shutterstock.com: 4; Kirillo-Belozersky Monastery: 15; Marina M/Pexels: 46; Tom Milner-Gulland: 11; National Library of Russia, St Petersburg: 18, 19, 24, 54; after B. A. Ognev, 'The Assumption Cathedral on the Gorodok in Zvenigorod', in *Materials and Studies in Archaeology of the USSR* (MIA), vol. XLIV (1955): 55; Russian State Library, Moscow: 25, 30, 31; State Hermitage Museum, St Petersburg: 6; State Russian Museum, St Petersburg: 5, 16; State Tretyakov Gallery, Moscow: 2, 3, 26, 27, 28, 29, 34, 35, 37, 50, 51, 57; Trinity Lavra of St Sergius, Sergiev Posad: 1, 9, 10, 20, 21; Vologda State Museum: 14.